DILEMMAS OF CHANGE

IN SOVIET POLITICS

DILEMMAS OF CHANGE
IN SOVIET POLITICS

Edited by
Zbigniew Brzezinski

Columbia University Press

NEW YORK AND LONDON

1969

This book is sponsored by the Research Institute
on Communist Affairs, Columbia University

The Contributors

Zbigniew Brzezinski is Director of the Research Institute on Communist Affairs, Columbia University. His books include *Alternative to Partition* (1966), *Ideology and Power in Soviet Politics* (1967), and *The Soviet Bloc: Unity and Conflict* (1967).

Frederick Barghoorn is Professor of Political Science, Yale University, and author of *Politics in the USSR* (1966) and other books.

Arthur Schlesinger, Jr., is Albert Schweitzer Professor of the Humanities at City University of New York. In 1966 he received his second Pulitzer Prize for the book *A Thousand Days—John F. Kennedy in the White House* (1965).

Eugene Lyons, formerly United States correspondent in Russia from 1928 to 1934, is presently a Senior Editor of *Reader's Digest*. He is the author of *Stalin: Czar of All the Russias* (1940) and *The Red Decade* (1941).

Giorgio Galli is an Italian journalist and scholar, whose books include *Storia del Partito Comunista Italiano* (1953).

Robert Conquest is a British poet as well as a writer on Soviet affairs. His books include a study of the problem of Soviet leadership succession, *Russia after Khrushchev* (1965) and *The Great Terror* (1968).

Boris Meissner is currently Director of the Seminar for Politics and East European Law, University of Kiel. Among his books are *Russland unter Chruschtschow* (1960) and *Sowjetgesellschaft im Wandel* (1966).

Jayantanuja Bandyopadhyaya is a Reader in the Department of International Relations, Jadaupur University, Calcutta. He is the author of *Indian Nationalism versus International Communism* (1966).

Issac Don Levine, a veteran correspondent and writer on Russia for nearly half a century, is the author of, among other books, *I Rediscover Russia* (1964).

Ernst Halperin is currently Visiting Professor, Department of Political Science, at MIT, where he has been Research Associate in Communist Affairs, Center of International Studies, since 1962. Previously he had been a correspondent in Yugoslavia, Vienna, and Warsaw.

Joseph Clark, a former correspondent in the Soviet Union, is now a free-lance writer. He is the author of *The Challenge of Coexistence* (1965).

Alexander Bregman was Chief Editorial Writer for *The Polish Daily* (London), and a regular contributor to journals in Europe and the United States, including *East Europe* and *The Reporter.* He died in London in 1967.

Merle Fainsod is Director of the Harvard University Library as well as Professor of Government at Harvard. He is the author of *Smolensk under Soviet Rule* and *How Russia is Ruled.*

Arrigo Levi is special correspondent for *La Stampa.* Previously he had been foreign and diplomatic correspondent for *Corriere della Sera, Il Giorno,* and Italian State Radio-Television.

Preface

While teaching at Columbia University a mixed graduate-undergraduate course on Soviet politics, I put together and distributed to my class the essays which *Problems of Communism* published in the years 1966-1968 on the problems of change in the Soviet Union. I found from my students' reactions that the essays, both by raising a number of issues and by advancing criticisms of my own introductory contribution, provided an extraordinarily valuable pedagogic device. They made it easier to identify alternative prospects for the Soviet political system, the limitations of the different approaches, as well as the methods employed in reaching the various conclusions. As a result, I became increasingly convinced that wider distribution of these essays would be desirable.

The original discussion in *Problems of Communism* began with my article "The Soviet Political System—Transformation or Degeneration?" and with a review by Michel Tatu of Michel Garder's book, *L'Agonie du régime en Russie soviétique.* Since Mr. Tatu's essay was essentially a book review, it is not included here. A number of contributors, however, also commented briefly on Mr. Garder's book, and hence it may be useful to summarize his point of view. In essence, his argument was that the Soviet political system would experience a major upheaval, even a collapse, by 1970. Mr. Tatu, in his review, disagreeing with Mr. Garder, argued that the future of the Soviet system will be shaped by "a series of compromises, solving all the more or less serious but not necessarily violent crises that may arise" which eventually "would transform the regime into a more effective, if still dictatorial system of government."

I want to express my gratitude to all the authors for agreeing to make the appearance of this collection possible. My special thanks go to Mr. Abraham Brumberg, Editor of *Problems of Communism*, for stimulating this discussion, providing it with intellectual direction, and for giving us his permission to have it reproduced. My very warmest personal thanks go to Mrs. Christine Dodson, the Administrative Assistant of the Research Institute on Communist Affairs, who supervised the overall preparation of the essays for publication, to Miss Sonia Sluzar, who did the needed research and review of the material, and to Miss Michelle Elwyn and Mr. Myron Gutmann, who were responsible for making its appearance possible. Finally, I wish to note that all the participants agreed to my suggestion that the royalties from this collective endeavor be contributed to the United Negro College Fund.

April, 1969 *Zbigniew Brzezinski*

Contents

The Soviet Political System: Transformation or Degeneration

✳

ZBIGNIEW BRZEZINSKI

The Soviet Union has celebrated its 50th anniversary. In this turbulent and rapidly changing world, for a political system to survive half a century is an accomplishment in its own right and obvious testimony to its durability. There are not many major political structures in the world today that can boast of such longevity. The anniversary, however, provides an appropriate moment for a critical review of the changes that have taken place in the Soviet system, particularly in regard to such critical matters as the character of its top leadership, the methods by which its leaders acquire power, and the relationship of the Communist Party to society. Furthermore, the time is also ripe to inquire into the implications of these changes, especially in regard to the stability and vitality of the system.

The Leaders

Today Soviet spokesmen would have us believe that the quality of the top Communist leadership in the USSR has been abysmal. Of the forty-five years since Lenin, according to official Soviet history, power was exercised for approximately five years by leaders subsequently unmasked as traitors (although later the charge of treason was retroactively reduced to that of deviation); for almost twenty years it was wielded by a paranoiac mass-murderer who irrationally slew his best comrades and ignorantly guided Soviet war strategy by pointing his finger at a globe; and, most recently, for almost ten years, by a "harebrained" schemer given to tantrums and with a propensity for wild organizational experimentation. On the basis of that record, the present leadership lays claim to representing a remarkable departure from a historical pattern of singular depravity.

While Soviet criticism of former party leaders is now abundant, little intellectual effort is expended on analyzing the implications of the changes in leadership. Yet that, clearly, is the important question insofar as the political system is concerned.

Lenin was a rare type of political leader, fusing in his person several functions of key importance to the working of a political system: he acted as the chief ideologist of the system, the principal organizer of the party (indeed, the founder of the movement), and the top administrator of the state. It may be added that such personal fusion is typical of early revolutionary leaderships, and today is exemplified by Mao Tse-tung. To his followers, Lenin was clearly a charismatic leader, and his power (like Hitler's or Mao Tse-tung's) depended less on institutions than on the force of his personality and intellect. Even after the Revolution, it was his personal authority that gave him enormous power, while the progressive institutionalization of Lenin's rule (the Cheka, the appearance of the *apparat*, etc.) reflected more the transformation of a revolutionary party into a ruling one than any significant change in the character of his leadership.

Lenin's biographers[1] agree that here was a man characterized by total political commitment, by self-righteous conviction, by tenacious determination, and by an outstanding ability to formulate intellectually appealing principles of political action as well as popular slogans suitable for mass consumption. He was a typically revolutionary figure, a man whose genius can be consummated only at that critical juncture in history when the new breaks off—and not just evolves —from the old. Had he lived a generation earlier, he probably would have died in a Siberian *taiga*; a generation later, he probably would have been shot by Stalin.

Under Stalin, the fusion of leadership functions was continued, but this was due less to his personal qualities as such than to the fact that, with the passage of time and the growing toll of victims, his power became nearly total and was gradually translated also into personal authority. Only a mediocre ideologist—and certainly inferior in that respect to his chief rivals for power—Stalin became institutionally the ideologue of the system. A dull speaker, he eventually acquired the "routinized charisma"[2] which, after Lenin's death, became invested in the Communist Party as a whole (much as the Pope at one time acquired the infallibility that for a long time had rested in the collective church). But his power

[1] Angelica Balabanoff, *Impressions of Lenin*, Ann Arbor, University of Michigan Press, 1964. Louis Fischer, *Life of Lenin*, New York, Harper, 1964. S. Possony, *Lenin, the Compulsive Revolutionary*, Chicago, Regnery, 1964. Bertram D. Wolfe, *Three Who Made a Revolution*, New York, Dial Press, 1948.

[2] For a discussion of "routinized charisma," see Amitai Etzioni, *A Comparative Analysis of Complex Organizations*, Glencoe, Ill., Glencoe Free Press, 1961, pp. 26 ff.

was increasingly institutionalized bureaucratically, with decision-making centralized at the apex within his own secretariat, and its exercise involved a subtle balancing of the
principal institutions of the political system: the secret police,
the party, the state, and the army (roughly in that order of
importance). Even the ostensibly principal organ of power,
the Politburo, was split into minor groups, "the sextets," the
"quartets," etc., with Stalin personally deciding who should
participate in which subgroup and personally providing (and
monopolizing) the function of integration.

If historical parallels for Lenin are to be found among the
revolutionary tribunes, for Stalin they are to be sought among
the Oriental despots.[3] Stalin, thriving on intrigue, shielded
in mystery, and isolated from society, wielded immense power
which reflected the immense tasks he succeeded in imposing
on his followers and subjects. Capitalizing on the revolutionary momentum and the ideological impetus inherited
from Leninism, and wedding it to a systematic institutionalization of bureaucratic rule, he could set in motion a social
and political revolution which weakened all existing institutions save Stalin's own secretariat and his chief executive arm,
the secret police. His power grew in proportion to the degree
to which the major established institutions declined in vitality
and homogeneity.[4]

[3] Compare the types discussed by J. L. Talmon in his *Political Mes-
sianism: the Romantic Phase*, New York, Praeger, 1960, with Barrington
Moore, Jr., *Political Power and Social Theory*, Cambridge, Mass., Harvard University Press, 1958, especially Chapter 2 on "Totalitarian Elements in Pre-Industrial Societies," or Karl Wittfogel, *Oriental Despotism*, New Haven, Yale University Press, 1957.

[4] It seems that these considerations are as important to the understanding of the Stalinist system as the psychopathological traits of Stalin
that Robert C. Tucker rightly emphasizes in his "The Dictator and
Totalitarianism," *World Politics*, July 1965.

The war, however, as well as the postwar reconstruction, produced a paradox. While Stalin's personal prestige and authority were further enhanced, his institutional supremacy relatively declined. The military establishment naturally grew in importance; the enormous effort to transfer, reinstall, and later reconstruct the industrial economy invigorated the state machinery; the party *apparat* began to perform again the key functions of social mobilization and political integration. But the aging tyrant was neither unaware of this development nor apparently resigned to it. The Byzantine intrigues resulting in the liquidation of the Leningrad leadership and Voznesenski, the "doctors' plot" with its ominous implications for some top party, military, and police chiefs, both clearly augured an effort to weaken any institutional limits on Stalin's personal supremacy.

Khrushchev came to power ostensibly to save Stalinism, which he defined as safeguarding the traditional priority of heavy industry and restoring the primacy of the party. In fact, he presided over the dismantling of Stalinism. He rode to power by restoring the predominant position of the party *apparat*. But the complexities of governing (as contrasted to the priorities of the power struggle) caused him to dilute the party's position. While initially he succeeded in diminishing the political role of the secret police and in weakening the state machinery, the military establishment grew in importance with the continuing tensions of the cold war.[5] By the time Khrushchev was removed, the economic priorities had become blurred because of pressures in agriculture and the

[5] For a good treatment of Soviet military debates, see Thomas Wolfe, *Soviet Strategy at the Crossroads*, Cambridge, Mass., Harvard University Press, 1964.

consumer sector, while his own reorganization of the party into two separate industrial and rural hierarchies in November 1962 went far toward undermining the party's homogeneity of outlook, apart from splitting it institutionally. Consequently, the state bureaucracy recouped, almost by default, some of its integrative and administrative functions. Khrushchev thus, perhaps inadvertently, restored much of the institutional balance that had existed under Stalin, but without ever acquiring the full powers of the balancer.

Khrushchev lacked the authority of Lenin to generate personal power, or the power of Stalin to create personal authority—and the Soviet leadership under him became increasingly differentiated. The top leader was no longer the top ideologist, in spite of occasional efforts to present Khrushchev's elaborations as "a creative contribution to Marxism-Leninism." The ruling body now contained at least one professional specialist in ideological matters, and it was no secret that the presence of the professional ideologue was required because someone had to give professional ideological advice to the party's top leader. Similarly, technical-administrative specialization differentiated some top leaders from others. Increasingly Khrushchev's function—and presumably the primary source of his still considerable power—was that of providing political integration and impetus for new domestic or foreign initiatives in a political system otherwise too complex to be directed and administered by one man.

The differentiation of functions also made it more difficult for the top leader to inherit even the "routinized charisma" that Stalin had eventually transferred to himself from the party as a whole. Acquiring charisma was more difficult for a leader who (even apart from a personal style and vulgar appearance that did not lend themselves to "image building") had neither the great "theoretical" flare valued by a movement that still prided itself on being the embodiment of a messianic ideology, nor the technical expertise highly regarded in a state which equated technological advance with human progress. Moreover, occupying the posts of First Secretary and Chairman of the Council of Ministers was not enough to develop a charismatic appeal since neither post had been sufficiently institutionalized to endow its occupant with the special prestige and aura that, for example, the President of the United States automatically gains on assuming office.

Trying to cope with this lack of charismatic appeal, Khrushchev replaced Stalin's former colleagues. In the process, he gradually came to rely on a younger generation of bureaucratic leaders to whom orderliness of procedure was instinctively preferable to crash campaigns. Administratively, however, Khrushchev was a true product of the Stalinist school, with its marked proclivity for just such campaigns at the cost of all other considerations. In striving to develop his own style of leadership, Khrushchev tried to emulate Lenin in stimulating new fervor and Stalin in mobilizing energies, but without the personal and institutional assets that each had commanded. By the time he was removed, Khrushchev had become an anachronism in the new political context he himself had helped to create.

Brezhnev and Kosygin mark the coming to power of a new generation of leaders, irrespective of whether they will for long retain their present positions.[6] Lenin's, Stalin's, and Khrushchev's formative experience was the unsettled period of conspiratorial activity, revolution, and—in Khrushchev's

[6] See S. Bialer, "An Unstable Leadership," *Problems of Communism*, July-August 1965.

case—civil war and the early phase of Communism. The new leaders, beneficiaries of the revolution but no longer revolutionaries themselves, have matured in an established political setting in which the truly large issues of policy and leadership have been decided. Aspiring young bureaucrats, initially promoted during the purges, they could observe—but not suffer from—the debilitating consequences of political extremism and unpredictable personal rule. To this new generation of clerks, bureaucratic stability—indeed, bureaucratic dictatorship—must seem to be the only solid foundation for effective government.

Differentiation of functions to these bureaucrats is a norm, while personal charisma is ground for suspicion. The new Soviet leadership, therefore, is both bureaucratic in style and essentially impersonal in form. The curious emphasis on *kollektivnost rukovodstva* (collectivity of leadership) instead of the traditional *kollektivnoe rukovodstvo* (collective leadership)—a change in formulation used immediately after Khrushchev's fall—suggests a deliberate effort at achieving not only a personal but also an institutional collective leadership, designed to prevent any one leader from using a particular institution as a vehicle for obtaining political supremacy.

The question arises, however, whether this kind of leadership can prove effective in guiding the destiny of a major state. The Soviet system is now led by a bureaucratic leadership from the very top to the bottom. In that respect, it is unique. Even political systems with highly developed and skillful professional political bureaucracies, such as the British, the French, or that of the Catholic Church, have reserved some top policy-making and hence power-wielding positions for non-bureaucratic professional politicians, presumably on the assumption that a free-wheeling, generalizing and competitive political experience is of decisive importance in shaping effective national leadership.

To be sure, some top Soviet leaders do acquire such experience, even in the course of rising up the bureaucratic party ladder, especially when assigned to provincial or republican executive responsibilities. There they acquire the skills of initiative, direction, integration, as well as accommodation, compromise, and delegation of authority, which are the basic prerequisites for executive management of any complex organization.

Nonetheless, even when occupying territorial positions of responsibility, the *apparatchiki* are still part of an extremely centralized and rigidly hierarchical bureaucratic organization, increasingly set in its ways, politically corrupted by years of unchallenged power, and made even more confined in its outlook than is normally the case with a ruling body by its lingering and increasingly ritualized doctrinaire tradition. It is relevant to note here (from observations made in Soviet universities) that the young men who become active in the Komsomol organization and are presumably embarking on professional political careers are generally the dull conformists. Clearly, in a highly bureaucratized political setting, conformity, caution, and currying favor with superiors count for more in advancing a political career than personal courage and individual initiative.[7]

7 Writing about modern bureaucracy, V. A. Thompson (*Modern Organization*, New York, Knopf, 1961, p. 91) observed: "In the formally structured group, the idea man is doubly dangerous. He endangers the established distribution of power and status, and he is a competitive threat to his peers. Consequently, he has to be suppressed." For a breezy treatment of some analogous experience, see also, E. G. Hegarty, *How to Succeed in Company Politics*, New York, McGraw-Hill, 1963.

Such a condition poses a long-range danger to the vitality of any political system. Social evolution, it has been noted, depends not only on the availability of creative individuals, but also on the existence of clusters of creators who collectively promote social innovation. "The ability of any gifted individual to exert leverage within a society . . . is partly a function of the exact composition of the group of those on whom he depends for day-to-day interaction and for the execution of his plans."[8] The revolutionary milieu of the 1920s and even the fanatical Stalinist commitment of the 1930s fostered such clusters of intellectual and political talent. It is doubtful that the CPSU party schools and the Central Committee personnel department encourage, in Margaret Mead's terms, the growth of clusters of creativity, and that is why the transition from Lenin to Stalin to Khrushchev to Brezhnev probably cannot be charted by an ascending line.

This has serious implications for the Soviet system as a whole. It is doubtful that any organization can long remain vital if it is so structured that in its personnel policy it becomes, almost unknowingly, inimical to talent and hostile to political innovation. Decay is bound to set in, while the stability of the political system may be endangered, if other social institutions succeed in attracting the society's talent and begin to chafe under the restraints imposed by the ruling but increasingly mediocre *apparatchiki.*

The Struggle for Power

The struggle for power in the Soviet political system has certainly become less violent. The question is, however: Has it

[8] Margaret Mead, *Continuities in Cultural Evolution*, New Haven, Yale University Press, 1964, p. 181. See also the introduction, especially p. xx.

become less debilitating for the political system? Has it become a more regularized process, capable of infusing the leadership with fresh blood? A closer look at the changes in the character of the competition for power may guide us to the answer.

Both Stalin and Khrushchev rode to power by skillfully manipulating issues as well as by taking full advantage of the organizational opportunities arising from their tenure of the post of party First Secretary. It must be stressed that the manipulation of issues was at least as important to their success as the organizational factor, which generally tends to receive priority in Western historical treatments. In Stalin's time, the issues facing the party were, indeed, on a grand scale: world revolution *vs.* socialism in one country; domestic evolution *vs.* social revolution; a factionalized *vs.* a monolithic party. Stalin succeeded because he instinctively perceived that the new *apparatchiki* were not prepared to sacrifice themselves in futile efforts to promote foreign revolutions but—being for the most part genuinely committed to revolutionary ideals—were becoming eager to get on with the job of creating a socialist society. (Moreover, had the NEP endured another ten years, would the Soviet Union be a Communist dictatorship today?)

Stalin's choice of socialism in one country was a brilliant solution. It captivated, at least in part, the revolutionaries; and it satisfied, at least partially, the accommodators. It split the opposition, polarized it, and prepared the ground for the eventual liquidation of each segment with the other's support. The violence, the terror, and finally the Great Purges of 1936-1938 followed logically. Imbued with the Leninist tradition of intolerance for dissent, engaged in a vast undertaking of social revolution that taxed both the resources and the nerves of party members, guided by an unscrupulous and

paranoiac but also reassuringly calm leader, governing a backward country surrounded by neighbors that were generally
hostile to the Soviet experiment, and increasingly deriving
its own membership strength from first-generation proletarians with all their susceptibility to simple explanations and
dogmatic truths, the ruling party easily plunged down the
path of increasing brutality. The leader both rode the crest
of that violence and controlled it. The terror never degen-
erated into simple anarchy, and Stalin's power grew immeas-
urably because he effectively practiced the art of leadership
according to his own definition:

The art of leadership is a serious matter. One must not lag behind
the movement, because to do so is to become isolated from the
masses. But neither must one rush ahead, for to rush ahead is to
lose contact with the masses. He who wants to lead a movement
and at the same time keep in touch with the vast masses must
wage a fight on two fronts—against those who lag behind and
those who run ahead.[9]

Khrushchev, too, succeeded in becoming the top leader
because he perceived the elite's predominant interests. Restoration of the primary position of the party, decapitation of
the secret police, reduction of the privileges of the state
bureaucrats while maintaining the traditional emphasis on
heavy industrial development (which pleased both the industrial elite and the military establishment)—these were
the issues which Khrushchev successfully utilized in the mid-
1950s to mobilize the support of officials and accomplish the
gradual isolation and eventual defeat of Malenkov.

But the analogy ends right there. The social and even the
political system in which Khrushchev came to rule was rela-

[9] J. V. Stalin, *Problems of Leninism*, Moscow, 1940, p. 338.

tively settled. Indeed, in some respects, it was stagnating, and Khrushchev's key problem, once he reached the political apex (but before he had time to consolidate his position there) was how to get the country moving again. The effort to infuse new social and political dynamism into Soviet society, even while consolidating his power, led him to a public repudiation of Stalinism which certainly shocked some officials; to sweeping economic reforms which disgruntled many administrators; to a dramatic reorganization of the party which appalled the *apparatchiki*; and even to an attempt to circumvent the policy-making authority of the party Presidium by means of direct appeals to interested groups, which must have both outraged and frightened his colleagues. The elimination of violence as the decisive instrumentality of political competition—a move that was perhaps prompted by the greater institutional maturity of Soviet society, and which was in any case made inevitable by the downgrading of the secret police and the public disavowals of Stalinism—meant that Khrushchev, unlike Stalin, could not achieve both social dynamism and the stability of his power. Stalin magnified his power as he strove to change society; to change society Khrushchev had to risk his power.

The range of domestic disagreement involved in the post-Stalin struggles has also narrowed with the maturing of social commitments made earlier. For the moment, the era of grand alternatives is over in Soviet society. Even though any struggle tends to exaggerate differences, the issues that divided Khrushchev from his opponents, though of great import, appear pedestrian in comparison to those over which Stalin and his enemies crossed swords. In Khrushchev's case, they pertained primarily to policy alternatives; in the case of Stalin, they involved basic conceptions of historical development. Compare the post-Stalin debates about the allocation of resources among different branches of the economy, for example, with the debates of the 1920s about the character and pace of Soviet industrialization; or Khrushchev's homilies on the merits of corn—and even his undeniably bold and controversial virgin lands campaign—with the dilemma of whether to collectivize a hundred million reticent peasants, at what pace and with what intensity in terms of resort to violence.

It is only in the realm of foreign affairs that one can perhaps argue that grand dilemmas still impose themselves on the Soviet political scene. The nuclear-war-or-peace debate of the 1950s and early 1960s is comparable in many respects to the earlier conflict over "permanent revolution" or "socialism in one country." Molotov's removal and Kozlov's political demise were to a large extent related to disagreements concerning foreign affairs; nonetheless, in spite of such occasional rumblings, it would appear that on the peace-or-war issue there is today more of a consensus among the Soviet elite than there was on the issue of permanent revolution in the 1920s. Although a wide spectrum of opinion does exist in the international Communist movement on the crucial questions of war and peace, this situation, as far as one can judge, obtains to a considerably lesser degree in the USSR itself. Bukharin *vs.* Trotsky can be compared to Togliatti *vs.* Mao Tse-tung, but hardly to Khrushchev *vs.* Kozlov.

The narrowing of the range of disagreement is reflected in the changed character of the cast. In the earlier part of this discussion, some comparative comments were made about Stalin, Khrushchev, and Brezhnev. It is even more revealing, however, to examine their principal rivals. Take the men who opposed Stalin: Trotsky, Zinoviev, and Bukharin. What a range of political, economic, historical, and intellectual creativity, what talent, what a diversity of personal characteristics and backgrounds! Compare this diversity with the strikingly uniform personal training, narrowness of perspective, and poverty of intellect of Malenkov, Kozlov, and Suslov.[10] A regime of the clerks cannot help but clash over clerical issues.

The narrowing of the range of disagreement and the cooling of ideological passions mean also the wane of political violence. The struggle tends to become less a matter of life or death, and more one in which the price of defeat is simply retirement and some personal disgrace. In turn, with the routinization of conflict, the political system develops even a body of precedents for handling fallen leaders. By now there must be a regular procedure, probably even some office, for handling pensions and apartments for former Presidium members, as well as a developing social etiquette for dealing with them publicly and privately.[11]

More important is the apparent development in the Soviet system of something which might be described as a regularly available "counter-elite." After Khrushchev's fall, his successors moved quickly to restore to important positions a num-

[10] One could hardly expect a historian to work up any enthusiasm for undertaking to write, say, Malenkov's biography: *The Apparatchik Promoted, the Apparatchik Triumphant, the Apparatchik Pensioned!*

[11] Can Mikoyan, for example, invite Khrushchev to lunch? This is not a trivial question, for social mores and political style are interwoven. After all, Voroshilov, who had been publicly branded as a military idiot and a political sycophant, was subsequently invited to a Kremlin reception. Zhukov, against whom the Bonapartist charge still stands, appeared in full regalia at the 20th anniversary celebration of the Soviet victory in World War II.

ber of individuals whom Khrushchev had purged,[12] while some of Khrushchev's supporters were demoted and transferred. Already for a number of years now, it has been fairly common practice to appoint party officials demoted from high office either to diplomatic posts abroad or to some obscure, out-of-the-way assignments at home. The total effect of this has been to create a growing body of official "outs" who are biding their time on the sidelines and presumably hoping someday to become the "ins" again. Moreover, they may not only hope; if sufficiently numerous, young, and vigorous, they may gradually begin to resemble something of a political alternative to those in power, and eventually to think and even act as such. This could be the starting point of informal factional activity, of intrigues and conspiracies when things go badly for those in power, and of organized efforts to seduce some part of the ruling elite in order to stage an internal change of guard.[13] In addition, the availability of an increasingly secure "counter-elite" is likely to make it more difficult for a leader to consolidate his power. This in turn might tend to promote more frequent changes in the top leadership, with policy failures affecting

---

[12] F. D. Kulakov, apparently blamed by Khrushchev in 1960 for agricultural failings in the RSFSR, was appointed in 1965 to direct the Soviet Union's new agricultural programs; V. V. Matskevich was restored as Minister of Agriculture and appointed Deputy Premier of the RSFSR in charge of agriculture; Marshal M. V. Zakharov was reappointed as Chief-of-Staff of the Armed Forces; even L. G. Melnikov reemerged from total obscurity as chairman of the industrial work safety committee of the RSFSR.

[13] Molotov's letter to the Central Committee on the eve of the 22nd Party Congress of October 1961, which bluntly and directly charged Khrushchev's program with revisionism, was presumably designed to stir up the *apparatchiki* against the First Secretary. It may be a portent of things to come.

the power of incumbents instead of affecting—only retroactively—the reputation of former leaders, as has hitherto been the case.

The cumulative effect of these developments has been wide-ranging. First of all, the reduced importance of both ideological issues and personalities and the increasing weight of institutional interests in the periodic struggles for power —a phenomenon which reflects the more structured quality of present-day Soviet life as compared with the situation under Stalin—tend to depersonalize political conflict and to make it a protracted bureaucratic struggle. Second, the curbing of violence makes it more likely that conflicts will be resolved by patched-up compromises rather than by drastic institutional redistributions of power and the reappearance of personal tyranny. Finally, the increasingly bureaucratic character of the struggle for power tends to transform it into a contest among high-level clerks and is therefore not conducive to attracting creative and innovating talent into the top leadership.

Khrushchev's fall provides a good illustration of points made above, as well as an important precedent for the future. For the first time in Soviet history, the First Secretary was toppled by his associates. This was done not in order to replace him with an alternative personal leader or to pursue genuinely alternative goals, but in order to depersonalize the leadership and to pursue more effectively many of the previous policies. In a word, the objectives were impersonal leadership and higher bureaucratic efficiency. Khrushchev's removal, however, also meant that personal intrigues and cabals can work, that subordinate members of the leadership—or possibly, someday, a group of ex-leaders—can effectively conspire against a principal leader, with the result that any future First Secretary is bound to feel far less secure than Khrushchev must have felt at the beginning of October 1964.

The absence of an institutionalized top executive officer in the Soviet political system, in conjunction with the increased difficulties in the way of achieving personal dictatorship and the decreased personal cost of defeat in a political conflict, create a ready-made situation for group pressures and institutional clashes. In fact, although the range of disagreement may have narrowed, the scope of elite participation in power conflicts has already widened. Much of Khrushchev's exercise of power was preoccupied with mediating the demands of key institutions, such as the army, or with overcoming the opposition of others, such as the objections of the administrators to economic decentralization or of the heavy industrial managers to non-industrial priorities. These interests were heavily involved in the Khrushchev-Malenkov conflict and in the "anti-party" episode of 1957.

At the present time, these pressures and clashes take place in an almost entirely amorphous context, without constitutional definition and established procedures. The somewhat greater role played by the Central Committee in recent years still does not suffice to give this process of bureaucratic conflict a stable institutional expression. As far as we know from existing evidence, the Central Committee still acted during the 1957 and 1964 crises primarily as a ratifying body, giving formal sanction to decisions already fought out in the Kremlin's corridors of power.[14] It did not act as either the arbiter or the supreme legislative body.

The competition for power, then, is changing from a death

[14] Roger Pethybridge, A Key to Soviet Politics, New York, Praeger, 1962. See also Myron Rush, The Rise of Khrushchev, Washington, D.C., Public Affairs Press, 1958.

struggle among the few into a contest played by many more. But the decline of violence does not, as is often assumed, automatically benefit the Soviet political system; something more effective and stable has to take the place of violence. The "game" of politics that has replaced the former mafia-style struggles for power is no longer murderous, but it is still not a stable game played within an established arena, according to accepted rules, and involving more or less formal teams. It resembles more the anarchistic free-for-all of the playground and therefore could become, in some respects, even more debilitating to the system. Stalin encouraged institutional conflict below him so that he could wield his power with less restraint. Institutional conflict combined with mediocre and unstable personal leadership makes for ineffective and precarious power.

Party and Group Interests

In a stimulating study of political development and decay, Samuel Huntington has argued that stable political growth requires a balance between political "institutionalization" and political "participation": that merely increasing popular mobilization and participation in politics without achieving a corresponding degree of "institutionalization of political organization and procedures" results not in political development but in political decay.[15] Commenting in passing on the Soviet system, he therefore noted that "a strong party is in the Soviet public interest" because it provides a stable institutional framework.[16]

[15] Samuel P. Huntington, "Political Development and Political Decay," *World Politics* (Princeton, N.J.) April 1965.
[16] *Ibid.*, p. 414.

The Soviet political system has certainly achieved a high index of institutionalization. For almost five decades the ruling party has maintained unquestioned supremacy over the society, imposing its ideology at will. Traditionally, the Communist system has combined its high institutionalization with high pseudo-participation of individuals.[17] But a difficulty could arise if division within the top leadership of the political system weakened political "institutionalization" while simultaneously stimulating genuine public participation by groups and institutions. Could this new condition be given an effective and stable institutional framework and, if so, with what implications for the "strong" party?

Today the Soviet political system is again oligarchic, but its socioeconomic setting is now quite different. Soviet society is far more developed and stable, far less *malleable* and atomized. In the past, the key groups that had to be considered as potential political participants were relatively few. Today, in addition to the vastly more entrenched institutional interests, such as the police, the military, and the state bureaucracy, the youth could become a source of ferment, the consumers could become more restless, the collective farmers more recalcitrant, the scientists more outspoken, the non-Russian nationalities more demanding. Prolonged competition among the oligarchs would certainly accelerate the assertiveness of such groups.

By now some of these groups have a degree of institutional

[17] The massive campaigns launching "public discussions" that involve millions of people, the periodic "elections" that decide nothing, were designed to develop participation without threat to the institutionalized political organization and procedures. The official theory held that as Communist consciousness developed and new forms of social and public relations took root, political participation would become more meaningful and the public would come to govern itself.

cohesion, and occasionally they act in concert on some issues.[18] They certainly can lobby and, in turn, be courted by ambitious and opportunistic oligarchs. Some groups, because of institutional cohesion, advantageous location, easy access to the top leadership, and ability to articulate their goals and interests, can be quite influential.[19] Taken together they represent a wide spectrum of opinion, and in the setting of oligarchical rule there is bound to be some correspondence between their respective stances and those of the top leaders. This spectrum is represented in simplified fashion by the chart on page 22, which takes cumulative account of the principal divisions, both on external and on domestic issues,

[18] A schematic distribution of these groups is indicated by the following approximate figures: (A) amorphous social forces that in the main express passively broad social aspirations: workers and peasants, about 88 million; white collar and technical intelligentsia, about 21 million. (B) specific interest groups that promote their own particular interests: the literary and artistic community, about 75 thousand; higher-level scientists, about 150 thousand; physicians, about 380 thousand. (C) policy groups whose interests necessarily spill over into broad matters of national policy: industrial managers, about 200 thousand; state and collective farm chairmen, about 45 thousand; commanding military personnel, about 80 thousand; higher-level state bureaucrats, about 250 thousand. These groups are integrated by the professional *apparatchiki*, who number about 150-250 thousand. All of these groups in turn could be broken down into subunits; for example, the literary community, institutionally built around several journals, can be divided into hard-liners, the centrists, and the progressives, etc. Similarly, the military. On some issues, there may be cross-interlocking of sub-groups, as well as more-or-less temporary coalitions of groups. See Z. Brzezinski and S. Huntington, *Political Power: USA-USSR*, New York, Viking Press, 1964, Ch. 4, for further discussion.

[19] An obvious example is the military command, bureaucratically cohesive and with a specific esprit de corps, located in Moscow, necessarily in frequent contact with the top leaders, and possessing its own journals of opinion (where strategic and hence also—indirectly—budgetary, foreign, and other issues can be discussed).

POLICY SPECTRUM USSR

Systemic Left		Marginalist Left		Centrist
Malenkov		Khrushchev Podgorny		Kosygin Mikoyan
			Regional apparat	
Consumer goods industry		Light industry		
				Military innovator
		Agronomists		
	Scientists			
Moscow-Leningrad intellectuals		Economic reformers (Liberman)		

that have perplexed Soviet political life during the last decade or so.[20] Obviously, the table is somewhat arbitrary and also highly speculative. Individuals and groups cannot be

[20] The categories "systemic left," etc., are adapted from R. R. Levine's book, *The Arms Debate* (Cambridge, Mass., Harvard University Press, 1963), which contains a suggestive chart of American opinion on international issues. By "systemic left" is meant here a radical reformist outlook, challenging the predominant values of the existing system; by "systemic right" is meant an almost reactionary return to past values; the other three categories designate differences of degree within a dominant "mainstream."

In the chart above (unlike Levine's), the center position serves as a dividing line, and hence no one is listed directly under it. Malenkov is listed as "systemic left" because his proposals represented at the time a drastic departure from established positions. Molotov is labeled "systemic right" because of his inclination to defend the essentials of the Stalinist system in a setting which had changed profoundly since Stalin's death.

Centrist		Right		Systemic Right
Brezhnev		Kozlov		Molotov
	Shelepin	Suzlov		Kaganovich
		Voronov		
	Central apparat		Agitprop	
				Heavy industry
		Conventional army		
		Ministerial bureaucrats		Secret police
	Economic computators (Nemchinov)			

categorized so simply, and some clearly could be shifted left or right with equal cause, as indeed they often shift themselves. Nonetheless, the chart illustrates the range of opinion that exists in the Soviet system and suggests the kind of alliances, group competition, and political courtship that probably prevail, cutting vertically through the party organization. Not just Western but also Communist (although not as yet Soviet) political thinkers are coming to recognize more and more openly the existence of group conflict even in a Communist-dominated society. A Slovak jurist recently observed:

The social interest in our society can be democratically formed only by the integration of group interests; in the process of this integration, the interest groups protect their own economic and other social interests; this is in no way altered by the fact that everything appears on the surface as a unity of interests.[21]

The jurist went on to stress that the key political problem facing the Communist system is that of achieving integration of group interests.

Traditionally, this function of integration has been monopolized by the party, resorting—since the discard of terror —to the means of *bureaucratic arbitration*. In the words of the author just cited, "the party as the leading and directing political force fulfills its functions by resolving intra-class and inter-class interests." In doing so, the party generally has preferred to deal with each group bilaterally, thereby preventing the formation of coalitions and informal group consensus. In this way the unity of political direction as well as the political supremacy of the ruling party have been maintained. The party has always been very jealous of its "integrative" prerogative, and the intrusion on the political scene of any other group has been strongly resented. The party's institutional primacy has thus depended on limiting the real participation of other groups.

If, for one reason or another, the party were to weaken in the performance of this function, the only alternative to anarchy would be some *institutionalized process of mediation*, replacing the party's bureaucratic arbitration. Since, as noted, group participation has become more widespread, while the party's effectiveness in achieving integration has been lessened by the decline in the vigor of Soviet leadership and by the persistent divisions in the top echelon, the cre-

[21] M. Lakatos, "On Some Problems of the Structure of Our Political System," *Pravny obzor* (Bratislava), No. 1, 1965, as quoted in Gordon Skilling's illuminating paper, "Interest Groups and Communist Politics," read to the Canadian Political Science Association in June 1965.

ation and eventual formal institutionalization of some such process of mediation is gaining in urgency. Otherwise participation could outrun institutionalization and result in a challenge to the party's integrative function.

Khrushchev's practice of holding enlarged Central Committee plenums, with representatives of other groups present, seems to have been a step toward formalizing a more regular consultative procedure. (It also had the politically expedient effect of bypassing Khrushchev's opponents in the central leadership.) Such enlarged plenums provided a consultative forum, where policies could be debated, views articulated, and even some contradictory interests resolved. Although the device still remained essentially non-institutionalized and only *ad hoc*, consultative and not legislative, still subject to domination by the party *apparat*, it was nonetheless a response to the new quest for real participation that Soviet society has manifested and which the Soviet system badly needs. It was also a compromise solution, attempting to wed the party's primacy to a procedure allowing group articulation.

However, the problem has become much more complex and fundamental because of the organizational and ideological crisis in the party over its relevance to the evolving Soviet system. For many years the party's monopoly of power and hence its active intervention in all spheres of Soviet life could indeed be said to be "in the Soviet public interest." The party provided social mobilization, leadership, and a dominant outlook for a rapidly changing and developing society. But, in the main, that society has now taken shape. It is no longer malleable, subject to simple mobilization, or susceptible to doctrinaire ideological manipulation.

As a result, Soviet history in the last few years has been dominated by the spectacle of a party in search of a role. What is to be the function of an ideocratic party in a relatively complex and industrialized society, in which the structure of social relationships generally reflects the party's ideological preferences? To be sure, like any large sociopolitical system, the Soviet system needs an integrative organ. But the question is, What is the most socially desirable way of achieving such integration? Is a "strong" party one that dominates and interferes in everything, and is this interference conducive to continued Soviet economic, political, and intellectual growth?

In 1962 Khrushchev tried to provide a solution. The division of the party into two vertically parallel, functional organs was an attempt to make the party directly relevant to the economy and to wed the party's operations to production processes. It was a bold, dramatic, and radical innovation, reflecting a recognition of the need to adapt the party's role to a new state of Soviet social development. But it was also a dangerous initiative; it carried within itself the potential for political disunity as well as the possibility that the party would become so absorbed in economic affairs that it would lose its political and ideological identity. That it was rapidly repudiated by Khrushchev's successors is testimony to the repugnance that the reorganization must have stimulated among the professional party bureaucrats.

His successors, having rejected Khrushchev's reorganization of the party, have been attempting a compromise solution—in effect, a policy of "muddling through." On the one hand, they recognize that the party can no longer direct the entire Soviet economy from the Kremlin and that major institutional reforms in the economic sphere, pointing toward more local autonomy and decision-making, are indispensable.[22] (Similar tendencies are apparent elsewhere—for example, the stress on professional self-management in the military establishment.) This constitutes a partial and implicit acknowledgment that in some respects a party of total control is today incompatible with the Soviet public interest.

On the other hand, since obviously inherent in the trend toward decentralization is the danger that the party will be gradually transformed from a directing, ideologically-oriented organization to a merely instrumental and pragmatic body specializing in adjustment and compromise of social group aspirations, the party functionaries, out of a sense of vested interest, have been attempting simultaneously to revive the ideological vitality of the CPSU. Hence the renewed stress on ideology and ideological training; hence the new importance attached to the work of the ideological commissions; and hence the categorical reminders that "Marxist education, Marxist-Leninist training, and the ideological tempering of CPSU members and candidate members is the primary concern of every party organization and committee."[23]

[22] See the report delivered by A. Kosygin to the CC Plenum on Sept. 27, 1965, proposing the reorganization of the Soviet economy. Also his speech at a meeting of the USSR State Planning Committee, *Planovoe khoziaistvo* (Moscow) April 1965; and the frank discussion by A. E. Lunev, "Democratic Centralism in Soviet State Administration," *Sovetskoe gosudarstvo i pravo* (Moscow), No. 4, 1965.

[23] "Ideological Hardening of Communists" (editorial), *Pravda*, June 28, 1965. There have been a whole series of articles in this vein, stressing the inseparability of ideological and organizational work. For details of a proposed large-scale indoctrination campaign, see V. Stepakov, head of the Department of Propaganda and Agitation of the Central Committee of the CPSU, "Master the Great Teaching of Marxism-Leninism," *Pravda*, Aug. 4, 1965.

However, it is far from certain that economic decentralization and ideological "tempering" can be pushed forward hand in hand. The present leadership appears oblivious to the fact that established ideology remains vital only when ideologically motivated power is applied to achieve ideological goals. A gradual reduction in the directing role of the party cannot be compensated for by an increased emphasis on ideological semantics. Economic decentralization inescapably reduces the scope of the political-ideological and increases the realm of the pragmatic-instrumental. It strengthens the trend, publicly bemoaned by Soviet ideologists, toward depolitization of the Soviet elite.[24] A massive indoctrination campaign directed at the elite cannot operate in a "de-ideologized" socioeconomic context, and major efforts to promote such a campaign could, indeed, prompt the social isolation of the party, making its dogmas even more irrelevant to the daily concerns of a Soviet scientist, factory director, or army general. That in turn would further reduce the ability of the party to provide effective integration in Soviet society, while underscoring the party *apparatchik's* functional irrelevance to the workings of Soviet administration and technology.

If the party rejects a return to ideological dogmas and renewed dogmatic indoctrination, it unavoidably faces the prospect of further internal change. It will gradually become a loose body, combining a vast variety of specialists, engineers, scientists, administrators, professional bureaucrats,

[24] Stepakov, *ibid.*, explicitly states that in recent years "many comrades" who have assumed leading posts in the "directive aktivs" of the party have inadequate ideological knowledge, even though they have excellent technical backgrounds; and he urges steps against the "replacement" of party training "by professional-technical education."

agronomists, etc. Without a common dogma and without an active program, what will hold these people together? The party at this stage will face the same dilemma that the fascist and falange parties faced, and that currently confronts the Yugoslav and Polish Communists: in the absence of a large-scale domestic program of change, in the execution of which other groups and institutions become subordinated to the party, the party's domestic primacy declines and its ability to provide social-political integration is negated.

Moreover, the Soviet party leaders would be wrong to assume complacently that the narrowed range of disagreement over domestic policy alternatives could not again widen. Persistent difficulties in agriculture could someday prompt a political aspirant to question the value of collectivization; or the dissatisfaction of some nationalities could impose a major strain on the Soviet constitutional structure; or foreign affairs could again become the source of bitter internal conflicts. The ability of the system to withstand the combined impact of such divisive issues and of greater group intrusion into politics would much depend on the adaptations that it makes in its organization of leadership and in its processes of decision-making. Unless alternative mechanisms of integration are created, a situation could arise in which some group other than the top *apparat*—a group that had continued to attract talent into its top ranks and had not been beset by bureaucratically debilitating conflict at the top—could step forth to seek power; invoking the Soviet public interest in the name of established Communist ideals, and offering itself (probably in coalition with some section of the party leadership) as the only alternative to chaos, it would attempt to provide a new balance between institutionalization and participation.

The Threat of Degeneration

The Soviet leaders have recognized the need for institutional reforms in the economic sector in order to revitalize the national economy. The fact is that institutional reforms are just as badly needed—and even more overdue—in the political sector. Indeed, the effort to maintain a doctrinaire dictatorship over an increasingly modern and industrial society has already contributed to a reopening of the gap that existed in prerevolutionary Russia between the political system and the society, thereby posing the threat of the degeneration of the Soviet system.

A political system can be said to degenerate when there is a perceptible decline in the quality of the social talent that the political leadership attracts to itself in competition with other groups; when there is persistent division within the ruling elite, accompanied by a decline in its commitment to shared beliefs; when there is protracted instability in the top leadership; when there is a decline in the capacity of the ruling elite to define the purposes of the political system in relationship to society and to express them in effective institutional terms; when there is a fuzzing of institutional and hierarchical lines of command, resulting in the uncontrolled and unchanneled intrusion into politics of hitherto politically uninvolved groupings.[25] All of these indicators were discernible in the political systems of Tsarist Russia, the French Third Republic, Chiang Kai-shek's China, and Rakosi's Hungary. Today, as already noted, at least several are apparent in the Soviet political system.

[25] For a general discussion and a somewhat different formulation, see S. Huntington, "Political Development and Political Decay," pp. 415-17.

This is not to say, however, that the evolution of the Soviet system has inevitably turned into degeneration. Much still depends on how the ruling Soviet elite reacts. Policies of retrenchment, increasing dogmatism, and even violence, which—if now applied—would follow almost a decade of loosening up, could bring about a grave situation of tension, and the possibility of revolutionary outbreaks could not be discounted entirely. "Terror is indispensable to any dictatorship, but it cannot compensate for incompetent leaders and a defective organization of authority," observed a historian of the French revolution, writing of the Second Directory.[26] It is equally true of the Soviet political scene.

The threat of degeneration could be lessened through several adaptations designed to adjust the Soviet political system to the changes that have taken place in the now more mature society. First of all, the top policy-making organ of the Soviet system has been traditionally the exclusive preserve of the professional politician, and in many respects this has assured the Soviet political system of able and experienced leadership. However, since a professional bureaucracy is not prone to produce broad "generalizing" talents, and since the inherent differentiation of functions within it increases the likelihood of leaders with relatively much narrower specialization than hitherto was the case, the need for somewhat broader representation of social talent within the top political leadership, and not merely on secondary levels as hitherto, is becoming urgent. If several outstanding scientists, professional economists, industrial managers, and others were to be co-opted by lateral entry into the ruling Presidium, the progressive tranformation of the leadership into a regime

26 G. Lefebvre, *The French Revolution*, New York, Columbia University Press, 1965, Vol. II, p. 205.

of clerks could thereby be averted, and the alienation of other groups from the political system perhaps halted.

Second, the Soviet leaders would have to institutionalize a chief executive office and strive to endow it with legitimacy and stability. This would eventually require the creation of a formal and open process of leadership selection as well—probably—as a time limit on the tenure of the chief executive position. The time limit, if honored, would depersonalize power, while an institutionalized process of selection geared to a specific date—and therefore also limited in time—would reduce the debilitating effects of unchecked and protracted conflict in the top echelons of power.

The CPSU continues to be an ideocratic party with a strong tradition of dogmatic intolerance and organizational discipline. Today, less militant and more bureaucratic in outlook, it still requires a top catalyst, though no longer a personal tyrant, for effective operations. The example of the Papacy, or perhaps of Mexico, where a ruling party has created a reasonably effective system of presidential succession, offers a demonstration of how one-man rule can be combined with a formal office of the chief executive, endowed with legitimacy, tenure, and a formally established pattern of selection.

Any real institutionalization of power would have significant implications for the party. If its Central Committee were to become in effect an electoral college, selecting a ruler whom no one could threaten during his tenure, the process of selection would have to be endowed with considerable respectability. It would have to be much more than a mere ratification of an a priori decision reached by some bureaucratic cabal. The process would require tolerance for the expression of diverse opinions in a spirit free of dogmatism, a certain amount of open competition among rivals for power, and perhaps even the formation of informal coalitions—at least temporary ones. In a word, it would mean a break with the Leninist past, with consequences that would unavoidably spill over from the party into the entire system and society.

Third, increased social participation in politics unavoidably creates the need for an institutionalized arena for the mediation of group interests, if tensions and conflicts, and eventually perhaps even anarchy, are to be avoided. The enlarged plenums of the Central Committee were a right beginning, but if the Committee is to mediate effectively among the variety of institutional and group interests that now exist in Soviet society, its membership will have to be made much more representative and the predominance of party bureaucrats watered down. Alternatively, the Soviet leaders might consider following the Yugoslav course of creating a new institution for the explicit purpose of providing group representation and reconciling different interests. In either case, an effective organ of mediation could not be merely a front for the party's continued bureaucratic arbitration of social interests, as that would simply perpetuate the present dilemmas.

Obviously, the implementation of such institutional reforms would eventually lead to a profound transformation of the Soviet system. But it is the absence of basic institutional development in the Soviet political system that has posed the danger of the system's degeneration. It is noteworthy that the Yugoslavs have been experimenting with political reforms, including new institutions, designed to meet precisely the problems and dangers discussed here. Indeed, in the long run, perhaps the ultimate contribution to

Soviet political and social development that the CPSU can make is to adjust gracefully to the desirability, and perhaps inevitability, of its own gradual withering away. In the meantime, the progressive transformation of the bureaucratic Communist dictatorship into a more pluralistic and institutionalized political system—even though still a system of one-party rule—seems essential if its degeneration is to be averted.

Changes in Russia:
The Need for Perspectives

✳

FREDERICK C. BARGHOORN

This symposium confronts the difficult but rewarding task of evaluating several thoughtful studies pertaining in one degree or another to the Soviet future.

Before commenting in detail on the fundamental issues posed by the studies in question, especially Professor Brzezinski's ingenious and original analysis, I should identify my point of view. Since political systems are the product of men's experience, they can change when there are changes in the environment by which they have been shaped. When political structures and the belief systems which legitimate them cease to be "functional," tensions develop between them and their internal and external environments. Institutions and practices which become obsolete must either be modified or replaced by new ones more appropriate to the tasks which confront them. Of course, political behavior is influenced not only by the experience of the living but also to some degree by living memories of the experiences of earlier generations. Hence, practices which have outlived much of their earlier relevance may, because of historical inertia, persist for a very long time indeed.[1] The concept of the political system as a set of interdependent processes and structures, adapting to but also influencing its domestic and foreign environments, is of course no magic key to political analysis. Its usefulness in the study of any system depends upon scrupulous regard for the unique history and characteristics of the particular system examined.

I shall comment briefly on the essays in the "Progress and Ideology" issue of *Problems of Communism* (Jan.-Feb., 1966). These competent surveys of post-Stalin developments in several fields of social and natural sciences suggest, in my opinion, that the Soviet "creative intelligentsia" is an increasingly autonomous and politically influential subcommunity of the overall political community. However, Soviet intellectuals are still constrained to seek limited objectives, pursued largely by such indirect means as behind-the-scenes pleading with party overseers, who are sometimes inclined for various reasons to support particular aspirations of the intelligentsia. The limited but real progress toward intellectual freedom made by the groups whose problems and prospects are examined in these essays tends to confirm Robert C. Tucker's view that the contemporary Soviet political system, having at least partly shaken off the heritage of the unique pressures of Stalin's personal rule, "should be pronounced,

[1] A tentative application of these concepts to the USSR was made by this author in "Soviet Russia: Orthodoxy and Adaptiveness," (see Lucian W. Pye and Sidney Verba, eds. *Political Culture and Political Development*, Princeton, N.J., Princeton University Press, 1965, pp. 450-511). A book by this writer on Soviet politics, applying the "political culture" and "political system" concepts to the Soviet Union, is *Politics in the USSR* (Boston, Little, Brown and Co., 1966).

at least provisionally, post-totalitarian."[2] Still, the continued, if diminishing, frustration by the party and state of unfettered intellectual inquiry and artistic expression—especially Moscow's obstructiveness toward the practical application of innovative thinking—indicates how vigilantly the party still shepherds "its" intellectuals. The satisfaction of Soviet liberal intellectuals—and their well-wishers abroad—with post-Stalin gains must be tempered by realization that these gains are still not protected by firm legal guarantees or even by explicit revisions of obsolete and stifling ideological dogmas. Some of the partial reforms granted by the Soviet Establishment were, after all, reluctant, possibly temporary concessions, impelled by domestic economic difficulties and by expediential foreign policy calculations as the desire to achieve respectability in the eyes of leftist French and Italian intellectuals.[3]

Brzezinski's brilliant article may well signal a new stage in Western analysis of Soviet politics. It deserves most careful scrutiny. Brzezinski combines systematic analysis of the development and present state of the Soviet policy with provocative forecasts of its various possible futures. Forecasting the political future is hazardous, and many scholars regard it as an idle exercise. However, the hypothetical futures forecast by Brzezinski have considerable value in helping to orient us toward various contingencies. Moreover, they may spur us to a sharp look at the warp of the past in search of intimations of the woof of the future. Brzezinski avoids overcommitment to a particular hypothesis by making his predictions

[2] Robert C. Tucker, "The Dictator and Totalitarianism," *World Politics* (Princeton, N.J.), Vol. XVII, No. 4, pp. 555-83, esp. p. 571.
[3] On the latter point, see Priscilla Johnson, *Khrushchev and the Arts*, Cambridge, Mass., Harvard University Press, 1965, pp. 62-64.

contingent upon a variety of possible conditions. However, I think that his use of the "ideal type" mode of analysis, which for clarity and effectiveness selects aspects of a problem considered particularly significant, leads to some oversimplification. I share what I regard as his underlying assumption that a political system designed for the conduct and consolidation of a revolution is not necessarily suited to the needs of a relatively modernized society. The latter may be most simply characterized as a society whose members would like fewer jails and jailers, more comforts and conveniences, less propaganda and more uncensored information.

Brzezinski frames his analysis largely in terms of the concepts of political "degeneration," or decay, and "institutionalization," a proper level and quality of which he regards as essential to the constructive guidance and control of the emerging demands of productive social groups for access to the making of national policy. I agree with Brzezinski that important adjustments, and perhaps fundamental reforms, are necessary if the Soviet Union is to preserve stability and achieve continued dynamic growth in popular welfare. I believe also that without such reforms the USSR will eventually lose ground in international competition.

However, it seems to me that Brzezinski exaggerates the clear and present danger of "degeneration" in the Soviet political system. Incidentally, or perhaps not so incidentally, it is very difficult to gather from Brzezinski's article any very precise indication of just when political decay began to set in and how far it has proceeded or will, within any specific period of time, develop. Possibly Brzezinski will wish in the future to further refine his predictive techniques.

Second, Brzezinski's somewhat schematic use of the concept of institutionalization leads him to exaggerate the imminence of decay, and to underestimate the difficulties of institutionalizing the fundamental reforms which he regards as antidecay prophylactics. The reforms which he suggests are so fundamental as to amount, in effect, to the adoption by Soviet Communists of some sort of limited parliamentary or constitutional regime. Certainly this would be highly desirable, but how likely is it to occur in the foreseeable future?

The Russian political tradition is woefully defective in the prerequisites for gradualism. Russia's tragic history hinders the acquisition of a mature, balanced political character. Both the Tsarist and the Soviet political cultures have exalted the virtues of a stern social discipline and of unquestioned acceptance of the ruler's commands by his subjects. Most Russian citizens, in my opinion, are still so awed by authority and so unsophisticated politically as to be easily manipulated or at best cowed by a display of determination from on high. In the Soviet era especially, citizens have been heavily indoctrinated in an anti-liberal spirit not calculated to foster sympathy for a wide sharing of authority and responsibility among even highly placed elite groups, and still less receptive to notions of governmental responsiveness to the wishes of the "masses." The elite elements are probably united both against internal subversion of their privileges and against "imperialist" threats from abroad. If the present Soviet political system disintegrates within the next few years, it will probably be replaced at least for some time by a nationalistic oligarchy, representing a coalition of forces, dominated by moderate, production-oriented party leaders, scientists, industrialists, and military figures. However, I think that the more desirable outcome envisaged by Brzezinski as one of his hypothetical variants, namely, gradual constitutional development, might eventuate after a long period of international tranquility and increasingly rewarding Soviet contact with the West.

In my opinion, fundamental change—or collapse—can occur only when at least the following conditions exist. First, the leadership must be badly split, or paralyzed by indecision. Second, there must be widespread loss of respect and support for the political authorities. Finally, it must become possible for some sort of organized political opposition with a clear conception of an alternative to the present system to organize, covertly or overtly, for effective political action. It seems reasonable to assume that some years will pass before these conditions are fulfilled.

Moreover, it will probably be possible to make partial reforms, short of those suggested by Professor Brzezinski, which will enable the present Soviet political system to continue to function fairly effectively for at least another ten or fifteen years. I am not persuaded that it would be impossible to retain the present centralized system of policy formation for some time, while granting increasing autonomy to the economic bureaucracy, to the scientific community, and beyond. Also, within the party itself, improved training and a more efficient method of recruitment of party executives, especially those assigned to coordinating the efforts of and maintaining liaison with the leaders of the various professional communities, could go far toward gaining increased support for the political authorities. To the extent that the party can recruit top executives capable of perceiving early enough the need for adjustments and taking initiatives to make them before pressures become explosive, it may be able to survive, and even to flourish. The burden of proof is upon anyone who takes the view that the Soviet political elite has lost or will soon lose the touch that has enabled it to perform its functions thus far with a relatively high degree of effectiveness. It is not irrelevant to note that the post-Khrushchev leadership, despite its perhaps excessive caution, has taken important steps toward improving the relationship between the political system and the Soviet national economy. If the reforms instituted at the September 1965 plenum prove successful, the economy, and indirectly the political system, will be considerably strengthened— even though the uneasy compromise effected at the plenum between centralized organization and managerial autonomy is likely to fail.

In foreign affairs, at least, the Brezhnev-Kosygin leadership has displayed considerable skill in steering a course between the other two giants of the international arena, Communist China and the United States. Kosygin, in particular, seems a more skillful diplomat than any of us would have predicted before his mediation between India and Pakistan.

Despite my reservations, I agree with Brzezinski that existing Soviet political structures and the ideology which serves as a major source of their legitimacy are increasingly irrelevant to a more and more diversified society. Whether or not the specific institutional changes he regards as necessary for the effective processing of social demands by the polity are necessary or feasible remains largely unpredictable. There are so many unknowns and unknowables. For example, how sure can we be that a dynamic leader may not arise in the coming years—or months—to replace the colorless Brezhnev-Kosygin team and once again get Soviet society moving?

We must beware of confusing the desirable with the real. Fundamental social and political changes usually occur slowly, unevenly, and in a zigzag fashion. Some parts of the system may change more rapidly, or more slowly, than others, although it is doubtless true that profound changes, for example, in the recruitment of leaders, eventually affect the functioning of all the structures of a system.

Institutional changes are usually preceded by broad changes in attitudes and ways of thinking. The erosion of ideological dogma among intellectuals is undoubtedly helping to undermine the psychological foundations of rule by a party which still makes a demigod of a man who died almost fifty years ago. There has recently been an encouraging revival of rational and empirical thinking in many fields. Its exponents, however, still constitute a small if growing minority, and they function in a considerable degree of isolation from one another. Still, empiricism, in science and social science, in economic administration and even in such fields as law, is increasingly challenging traditional Communist orthodoxy.[4] Related to these positive developments is the tendency for liberal, nonconformist Soviet writers to ally themselves with, and in a sense to act as spokesmen for, Soviet natural scientists—a trend symbolized by the fact that physicists are among the most generous patrons of avant-garde writing and "abstract" art.

However, the dominant political culture in which the rational, liberal factions of the Soviet intellectual community must cautiously maneuver is still characterized by a great deal of arbitrary administrative behavior, cloaked in secrecy

[4] In the field of law, see, for example, the remarkable article in *Izvestia* of Nov. 24, 1965, by the jurist V. Kudriavtsev, chiding the advocates of a "get-tough" policy toward criminals and urging empirical analysis as the only useful tool in analyzing the causes of crime.

and justified with sacrosanct dogma and official lies. I was vividly reminded of the seamy side of the political culture when on October 31, 1963, I was abducted on a Moscow street and detained in total isolation for nearly three weeks on a fabricated charge of military espionage.

The growing demand by various segments of the Soviet intellectual community for greater autonomy has forced the Kremlin to recognize grudgingly the need to relax controls over the trained and talented professionals upon whose willing and efficient performance national power depends. Concessions have even been made to that most troublesome group, the creative writers, at least to those not openly in opposition to official doctrine and policy.[5] Party spokesmen still warn that "groupism" (*gruppovshchina*) is incompatible with the proper behavior of Communist intellectuals, thus acknowledging the existence of group consciousness among professionals. However, Soviet social scientists, and even *Pravda* editorial writers, instruct researchers and youth leaders to take account in their work of the diversity of interests in Soviet society.[6]

There has been a great deal of behind-the-scenes bargaining between the Kremlin and the Soviet intelligentsia since the death of Stalin. One of its products has been the creation for the first time in the history of the USSR of the rudiments of a free, critical public opinion. Although still shackled, the Soviet intellectual community today is at least free to defend its views and interests against the cruder forms of arbi-

[5] The ground rules were provisionally set forth in A. Rumiantsev's article, "The Party and the Intelligentsia," *Pravda*, Feb. 21, 1965.

[6] See, for example: the article on "concrete" research by the prominent economist, V. Shubkin, in *Kommunist*, No. 3, 1965, and a *Pravda* editorial of June 16, 1965.

trary political interference, provided its members do not openly flout doctrines and symbols still regarded by the party leadership as above criticism. A poor sort of freedom? Yes, but almost unimaginable when measured by the Stalinist yardstick.

The possibility that the progress which has been achieved since the death of Stalin—toward personal security, the rule of law, limited intellectual freedom, and partial access to the exiting "bourgeois" world—might still be swept away by a relapse into Stalin-like terror seems remote, even if it cannot be completely excluded. In terms of a rational Kremlin approach to the Soviet national interest, the price of such a relapse would be prohibitively high. Its consequences could be dire for the lives and fortunes of many party and government leaders. It would cripple an increasingly sophisticated economy, and it could undermine support for Kremlin policies among important segments of Soviet society and among Western intellectuals, including many Communists.

The foregoing considerations seem to me to support the view that the Soviet political system will continue to adapt more or less successfully and positively to pressures arising in the intra-societal and extra-societal environments. It seems likely that the CPSU will be with us for a while before it accepts Professor Brzezinski's blithe recommendation that it wither away.[7]

[7] Perhaps it is needless to point out that party spokesmen still deny the possibility that the party can disappear before the achievement of Communism on a worldwide scale. See, for example, E. Bugaev and B. Leibzon, *Besedy ob ustave KPSS*, Moscow, 1964, p. 61.

A Muddling Evolution

*

ARTHUR SCHLESINGER, JR.

Zbigniew Brzezinski and Michel Garder have posed searching questions regarding the evolution of the Soviet political
system. Both writers know far more about the Soviet Union
than I do; and the only value of my comment must lie in
whatever diagnostic clues a historian can locate in the general processes of political change. My impression is that the
catastrophic prediction may well be unduly abstract and
apocalyptic. The Soviet regime, as Professor Brzezinski bril-
liantly shows, has unquestionably become increasingly an impersonal, bureaucratized, institutional order. But, while this
development no doubt places a premium on personal caution
and administrative routine and militates against political and
social invention, and while in other epochs and countries
such regimes have hardened into Byzantine rigidity, one
wonders whether this is likely to take place in an age characterized by high technological advance and in a state whose
power depends so vitally on science. In the last half of the
twentieth century, can a Soviet government, no matter what
its interior drift toward stagnation, turn its back on the need
for constant improvement in science and technology? And,

as it sees this need, will it not be compelled both to accept new ideas and to propitiate new groups?

Nazi Germany is often cited as proof of the compatibility of political regression and scientific progress. Yet it must not be forgotten that Hitler's Third Reich cultivated a condition of permanent tension and lasted only a dozen years: it always existed in a state of crisis. The Bolshevik revolution is reaching it first half-century, and the Soviet government shows many signs of middle age. Perhaps it is losing its old zest for living dangerously. Far from being what might be called a crisis state, it may well become, as indeed Professor Brzezinski suggests it is already, a "regime of the clerks."

Of course, external conditions might make it a crisis state again; and I would therefore think that along with the scientific environment of modern power, the international position of the Soviet Union must be taken into account before any sensible guess can be made about the future of the Soviet system. If the Soviet Union, in its competition with China for the leadership of the Communist world, should, for example, turn harshly against the West and relapse into the siege psychology of the 1920s and 1930s, the resurgence of tensions would undoubtedly rigidify the regime—though at the same time the revival of the crisis state might well reduce the claims of new groups on the regime for privileges and securities.

But, if the stumbling progress toward detente with the democratic world should go on, then will not the "clerks" continue to give ground, slowly and in bad temper, no doubt, but steadily all the same? A Stalin might have dared try by sheer force and cold brutality to stamp out the social consequences of economic modernization; but do perplexed pro-

vincial bureaucrats like Kosygin and Brezhnev have the de-
monic confidence and passion to wrench history out of its
tracks? Is there reason to suppose that, in the end, they will
be tougher at home than they are, for example, with M.
Ceausescu of Rumania?

Changes in ideas and institutions incited and required by
a high-technology age have been gathering force for some
years under the surface of Soviet society (as suggested by
the November-December 1965 issue of *Problems of Communism*). In certain respects the ideological overlay has perhaps become increasingly brittle and nominal. Conditions
of relative international stability might well speed this evolution. The phenomena mentioned by Professor Brzezinski
would seem to reinforce this possibility: the narrowing of the
range of disagreement, the cooling of ideological passions, the
waning of political violence, the emergence of a counter-elite.
The party, clinging to its power, would doubtless engage in
more or less frantic and sporadic rearguard actions designed
to revitalize authority and ideology; but, in the absence of
charismatic leadership, it would very likely take two steps
forward and one step back. The evolution would certainly
not go to the lengths of private enterprise or Western par-
liamentarism. There seems little reason, for example, *pace*
Djilas, to expect a two-party system in the Soviet Union.
But the CPSU might in due course become the Soviet equivalent of the Congress Party of India or the *Partido Revo-
lucionario Institucional* of Mexico—a loose central party, ab-
sorbing all the significant political tendencies within the society and working out its own methods of administration and
succession.

The great bureaucracies of history, if permitted sufficient
time, have often displayed a capacity for lumbering adapta-

tion. Given a world without major war, given a Soviet economy without major crisis, given the imperative of a scientific age, a muddling evolution would seem more likely to this historian than stark confrontation and upheaval.

The Realities of a Vision

✱

EUGENE LYONS

In a recent book, *L'Agonie du régime en Russie soviétique,* a long-time student of Soviet affairs, Michel Garder, argues that peaceful evolution of the Communist tyranny into something approximating freedom is impossible. He therefore foresees collapse in revolution—imprudently setting 1970 as the date for its consummation. Date aside, this is also the view of anti-Communist Russians like the poet-novelist Valery Tarsis, whose first message, on arriving in London to begin his life in exile at the age of 60, was that his native land was heading for revolution. It is the conclusion, too, of some non-Soviet observers of Kremlin communism, none of them, as far as I know, a certified academic Kremlinologist (or Sovietologist, as the case may be).

In reviewing the Garder book, with a passing allusion to Tarsis as well, Michel Tatu was almost apologetic for treating it seriously. He pointed out that the prognosis is not in line with the "scholarly treatises" to which experts on the USSR have accustomed us, and duly noted its "apocalyptic character." After all, he said, "it is not a bad idea occasionally to leave the beaten path and, even at the risk of over-simplification, to unfold a fearless vision of the future."

The implication of his cautious approach is that the scholarly treatises stick to the beaten path, fearful of conclusions that might seem apocalyptic-visionary, and hence unscholarly. Could disdain for the possibility of revolution be a built-in defense mechanism in the academic mind, protecting it against the sins of presumptive extremism?

Professor Barghoorn dismisses the Garder-Tarsis thesis as "the latest of a long line of apocalyptic predictions of the collapse of communism," warning that "great revolutions are most infrequent and that successful political systems are tenacious and adaptive."

But great revolutions *have* taken place (and not as infrequently as he assumes), despite the apocalyptic visions of those who sensed their coming. While the Soviet oligarchy is "tenacious" enough, Professor Barghoorn's own testimony raises considerable doubt that it is sufficiently "adaptive" to meet the current challenges. Moreover, except in terms of durability (all systems and regimes survive until they are overthrown), Soviet communism hardly rates as a "successful political system." Its conspicuous failure to achieve "legitimacy," if nothing else, refutes that judgment. His own observation that "the Russian political tradition is woefully defective in the prerequisites for gradualism" should have curbed his contempt for predictions of explosive, apocalyptic events.

Taken together, Barghoorn and Professor Brzezinski paint a picture that can be fairly called prerevolutionary, by analogy with the last stage of Tsarism or with Hungary on the eve of the October 1956 uprising. Should a popular revolution erupt in the Soviet Union, they will be able to point to these analyses as having identified the factors which precluded a non-violent solution. For they recognize, in their respective essays, that the Soviet leadership today is trapped by its ideological commitments and life-long habits of total power; that it is essentially mediocre and incapable of providing the necessary creative reforms, particularly in the political area, called for by its mounting troubles.

Yet they bypass the logic of their own findings, ending lamely with the assumption that despite its horrendous problems and difficulties the regime will somehow muddle through. Barghoorn concludes that "the Soviet political system will continue to adapt more or less successfully and positively" to the deepening pressures, and Brzezinski comes close to predicting that a parliamentary-constitutional system will magically emerge from the sorry plight he describes. Both forecasts seem to me more farfetched and unrealistic than the expectation of revolution.

Professor Brzezinski attests to the "decline in the vigor of Soviet leadership" and sees scant hope of its revitalization. The system, he shows, is "inimical to talent and hostile to political innovation . . . not conducive to attracting creative and innovative talent into its top leadership." Having exposed the "singular depravity" of their predecessors, the present hierarchs cannot even contemplate institutional reforms in the political sector, though these are "even more badly needed—and even more overdue" than in other sectors. "To this new generation of clerks," Brzezinski writes, "bureaucratic stability—indeed, bureaucratic dictatorship—must seem the only solid foundation for effective government."

Under these conditions, Brzezinski believes, " decay is bound to set in . . . the stability of the political system may be endangered." Meanwhile, the challenges of this ineffective power are likely to intensify—from youth in ferment, from restless consumers, from recalcitrant collective farmers, from more demanding non-Russian nationalities. He points to "indicators" of the kind "discernible in the political systems of Tsarist Russia, the French Third Republic, Chiang Kai-shek's China, and Rakosi's Hungary"—a reopening of "the gap that existed in prerevolutionary Russia between the political system and the society, thereby posing the threat of the degeneration of the Soviet system."

At this point the reader expects the professor to acknowledge the likelihood, if not the inevitability, of a breakdown of the system. But nothing of the sort. Brzezinski instead proceeds to prescribe a cellar-to-garret transformation of the Soviet political state if it is to be saved from utter "degeneration." Neither Brzezinski nor Barghoorn persuades us, or seems himself persuaded, that the creative innovating abilities needed for doing these things can be generated in time. Yet they cannot bring themselves to face up unambiguously to the possibilities of revolution.

Revolution has always seemed "impossible" and apocalyptic until it occurred, after which everyone sagely agreed that it was "inevitable." A week before the 1953 uprising in East Germany, not one political specialist would have dared predict such an event. In Hungary, we were assured until the moment of the explosion that all elements of potential revolt had been liquidated. From Petrograd, in the first months of 1917, foreign correspondents warned that the talk of revolution was premature.

I am not predicting a revolution against the Soviet dictatorship but underlining its possibility. It seems to me more reasonable to forecast a violent upheaval than to engage in the same kind of speculations that have been offered by Sovietologists convinced of the stability and durability of the present system. It is not without some significance that most of them are committed to "building bridges" to the hard-pressed Kremlin hierarchs, over the heads of the restive and fermenting population, to promote their hope of stability for all the world, as if their special assignment were to salvage the regime from the consequences of its own fallacies and crimes.

The history of the Soviet Union can be read as a permanent civil war between the rulers and the ruled, overt and military in the early years, covert but even more bloody ever since.[1] It would be an egregious error, at this stage of the conflict, to assume that the rulers have wide, let alone limitless, choices. The question is not merely how far they are willing to go to meet popular aspirations but how far they *can* go without risking their power and their lives. Partial reforms tend to lose their sedative qualities so long as the central disease of political dictatorship remains uncured. So-called liberalization and reform can proceed only to the point where it collides with the stone wall of the power monopoly, when a showdown of some sort is indicated.

In June, 1962, massive demonstrations against the Kremlin, touched off by the announcement of higher prices for meat and dairy products, took place in a number of cities and were crushed by military force. The bloodiest struggle occurred in Novocherkassk, about sixty miles from Rostov-

---

[1] For a detailed development of this assertion, see this author's *Our Secret Allies: the Peoples of Russia*, New York, Duell, Sloan and Pearce, 1954.

on-the-Don. The local militia proved inadequate and uncooperative. The first Soviet soldiers brought to the scene refused to shoot into the crowds. Finally, Moscow rushed in motorized units of KGB security troops which did the job of "pacification." An eye-witness now abroad writes that he counted more than 200 dead in the central square and that the toll was heavy in other parts of the city.[2] After the bloodbath, Mikoyan and Polianski flew to Novocherkassk with soothing words.

Such explosive events, all but a few successfully concealed by censorship, tell us things about the potentials for Russia's future that conventional analyses perhaps miss. Dissection in overly thin slices may blur awareness of the anatomy as a whole.

Barghoorn lists three "conditions" for collapse, meaning revolution: 1) the leadership must be badly split; 2) there must be "widespread loss of respect for the political authorities"; 3) there must be opposition organized for political action.

The second of these existed in Hungary before its revolution, as it exists today in the USSR. But the lack of the other two did not avert the great rebellion, supported almost unanimously by the people, the armed forces, and even elements in the ruling party itself. Hungary in 1956 may have set a classic pattern for the overthrow of totalitarian dictatorship. And the revolution, let us never forget, was thoroughly successful within its own frontiers—it had to be crushed from the outside. Were a comparable explosion to shatter the Soviet monolith, there would be no outside power to

[2] See "What Happened in Novocherkassk?" by Yevg. Elin, *Nashi Dnii*, No. 35, 1966 (Possev-Verlag, Frankfurt, Germany).

save the regime. That is, unless the West, which remained neutral in the Hungarian case, were to intervene on the Kremlin's side to safeguard its precious "bridges" in the name of stability.

A Bureaucracy Under Fire

*

GIORGIO GALLI

In the introductory essay to this volume, Professor Zbigniew Brzezinski observes:

The Soviet system is now controlled by a bureaucratic leadership from top to bottom. In that respect it is unique. Even political systems with highly developed . . . bureaucracies, . . . have reserved some top policy-making (and hence power-wielding positions) for non-bureaucratic professional politicians.

It is precisely this "unique" Soviet characteristic that makes it difficult to draw historical or sociological comparisons between the Soviet system and other systems or situations that do, after all, have something in common with the USSR of 1966. The difficulty of finding terms of comparison in turn makes the task of forecasting the future development of Soviet society particularly complex.

Michel Tatu writes in another contribution to the discussion: "It is not a bad idea occasionally to leave the beaten path and, even at the risk of oversimplification, to unfold a fearless vision of the future." Envisioning the future, however, requires as precise as possible an idea of what dynamic forces have already begun to operate in a particular system. In the Soviet situation our knowledge is somewhat limited; and while we must try to acquire an understanding of the forces at work, their role as "preceptors of the future" is made difficult by the enormous weight of the system's conservative structures. On the latter subject, Garder himself comments that "the most conservative Western bourgeois is a revolutionary next to the [Soviet] *apparatchik*." With less "oversimplification," Brzezinski maintains:

It is doubtful that any organization can long remain vital if it is so structured that in its personnel policy it becomes, almost unknowingly, inimical to talent and hostile to political innovation.

It is true that the more a political system keeps talent out of its structure, the more explosive force against the system will accumulate (the observations made by Pareto in this regard remain as valid as ever). On the other hand, a "unique" bureaucracy may also have unique capabilities to endure— that is to say, it may be able to maintain a certain system for quite a long period of time, despite the illogicality of its administration, and despite a conservatism so extreme that it paralyzes not only the political system but the entire society.

In the writer's opinion, Soviet Russia is nearing this stage of paralysis. The recent 23rd CPSU Congress exposed to public view a political class that is standing still. Few leaders addressed the Congress. China was barely mentioned. The names of Stalin and Khrushchev were not heard at all. Those who were instrumental in bringing about the downfall of Khrushchev did not even dare to claim credit for it, referring to the event in bureaucratic terms as "the Central Committee's decisions of October 1964." This peculiar attitude of silence indicates the extent of immobility that has taken hold of the all-powerful bureaucracy of the Soviet Union: it has lost not only the ability to act, but also the ability to speak.

Still, this enormous static mass dominates the scene, suffocating by its sheer weight every dynamic trend that makes itself felt in the Soviet Union. Among these trends, the one that has found most public expression—the intellectuals' attempt to describe the real Russia as against the nonexistent Russia of the official pamphlets—has so far been ruthlessly blocked. Yet such suppression takes its toll of the ruling bureaucracy. In order to understand this problem let us examine in turn the various dynamic forces at work in Soviet society.

History shows that talent, when shut off from the field of politics, often turns to the world of culture. Here different forms of talent can find room for expression, become polished, unite with one another, expound ideas, to the point of evolving into an indirect political force. This social process has been a familiar feature in closed societies: it operated throughout the Tsarist era in Russia and is still characteristic of the Communist regimes in Eastern Europe (consider, for example, the Hungarian situation of 1955-56 and that of Czechoslovakia today).

The intelligentsia, a Russian term expressing a Russian reality, has always been a cause of concern to Soviet leaders, as reflected in the recurring waves of repression launched by Stalin in the early 1930s, by Zhdanov in 1946, and by Khrushchev at the beginning of 1963, and by his successors just before and during the 23rd Congress. In spite of these repressions, the intelligentsia retains channels of communication with the citizenry and with public opinion, reaching some millions of people. In addition to the official magazines, there is a system of clandestine circulation. The intelligentsia also undoubtedly has contacts with university student groups, which (especially in Leningrad) appear to compose a social faction that exerts anti-bureaucratic pressure. Khrushchev was probably not bluffing when he remarked that if the "Petöfi clubs" (in which Hungarian intellectual dissent was centered) had been established in the USSR, he would have used a firm hand in repressing them. Therefore, we can surmise that the totalitarian bureaucracy must make use of a great deal of its static strength to subdue the intellectual opposition.

A second dynamic force in the USSR is composed of the managers of the enterprises, the technocrats. Their enemies are the same totalitarian political bureaucrats. Some of the talented people who turn their backs on politics because it rewards only conformism go into industry or take up a career in business. Having developed their capabilities and reached a certain managerial level, the technocrats find themselves confronted by an enormous and costly political bureaucracy which blocks every initiative or innovation. This group had a precedent in the "industrial party" that came into being during the final period of Lenin's life, but the conflict that ensued between political and industrial interests was stamped out with the launching of the Five-Year Plans, introducing Stalin's "command economy." Today there is no such simple solution, precisely because the centralized controlled economy can no longer promote the economic development of the USSR.

Even Stalin—along with Lenin and Trotsky—recognized that the spread of bureaucracy could pose a possible barrier to economic growth in the future. By the time Khrushchev had

entrenched himself in power, the huge bureaucratic structure—embracing millions of nonproductive persons receiv-
ing payment to make production more difficult—had long
since become a serious burden on the economy. Krushchev's
economic reforms of the late 1950s attempted to cope with
this problem, but they failed—mainly because the political
bureaucracy hampered their implementation and prevented
their success. In the process the needs of the business tech-
nocracy, today's "industrial party," were ignored.

The stronghold of political bureaucracy is, of course, the
party. Khrushchev's reform of the party structure (nowadays
treated as one of his gravest sins) was probably, at the end
of his parabolic rise, an attempt to demobilize the "sanctuaries" from which the totalitarian political bureaucracy was
firing point-blank against the economic reforms that he was
attempting to launch.

In the post-Khrushchev era, the exigencies of economic
development at first led the new regime to promise a decentralization reform that would increase the power of enterprise management; this promise was voiced by Kosygin
toward the end of 1964 and more decidedly in September
1965. Predictably, the type of reform proposed was attacked
by the Chinese Communists as a patent example of the
orientation of the "post-Khrushchev revisionists" toward
capitalism. Within the USSR the political bureaucracy obviously rallied its forces to fight back. At the 23rd CPSU
Congress in early 1966 Kosygin took a more cautious stand,
appearing to imitate the Khrushchevian tactic of two steps
forward and one step backward. Meanwhile, the party bureaucracy repealed the prudent rules of the 22nd Congress,
which had assured a minimum of internal regeneration
through a process of rotation in party offices.

Once again, then, the political bureaucracy is opening fire from its "sanctuaries" against economic reforms. But for this it will pay a high price: disorder and stagnation in the Soviet economy, waste, failure to make use of new energies and potential, and inability to satisfy the growing needs of consumers. How will the "industrial party" react against a party bureaucracy that is more conservative than the most conservative Western bourgeois, in that it blocks and paralyzes the economic development of the USSR? Most probably, the industrialists will keep pressing for application of the reforms that have been promised for the last ten years. We may assume, therefore, that the totalitarian bureaucracy will have to employ a great deal of its static strength to combat technocratic as well as intellectual pressure.

This same bureaucracy, so lacking in efficiency, so set against the intellectuals and the technocrats, must also take into account the grave problems of the international Communist movement. It must listen (though for the time being it is afraid to reply) to the very harsh accusations of the Chinese Communist Party. It faces continuing difficulties in its relations with the "people's democracies," arising out of such problems as the "austerity" program in Hungary, the increasingly independent attitude of Rumania, growing economic difficulties and intellectual ferment in Czechoslovakia, the struggle between the Gomulka regime and the Church, and the pressure on Ulbricht from West Germany. A conservative political bureaucracy whose only purpose is to enjoy its privileges in peace now finds itself continuously forced to face the problems of a world that is undergoing a process of rapid evolution.

The situations that have been summarized are relatively

well-known. They indicate where dynamic tendencies against bureaucratic immobilism may gain impetus—in the opposition of the intellectuals, in the needs of the technocrats, in the difficulties posed by mounting Chinese criticism and growing problems in the "people's democracies." But in addition, the political bureaucracy may find itself facing a storm that has received relatively little attention in forecasts.

At this point I will accept Michel Tatu's suggestion "to leave the beaten path," and offer some conjectures on how the bureaucratic political system might be affected by those elements that have brought about a great deal of change in the West in the last twenty-five years: mass consumption, mass education, mass communication, leisure time, leisure pursuits, even fashions. In a broad sense, the political influence of these elements has frequently been overlooked in the West, except for the superficial interpretation of a certain self-styled Marxist group, which maintains that all these elements were introduced surreptitiously by the capitalist bourgeoisie in order to lead the class-conscience of the proletarian masses astray.

Actually, mass consumption and communication, use of free time, styles in dancing and singing and dress—all these have contributed to creating what probably is the first "planetary" type of culture in the history of mankind, as the French sociologist Edgar Morin has defined it in *L'esprit du temps*. New cultural patterns that belong uniquely to the second half of the twentieth century predominate in all of the advanced industrial countries and have penetrated the so-called Third World. While they have been stopped at the borders of China, they have certainly infiltrated the Soviet Union.

In the USSR millions of young persons below the age of

30 attempt to follow, or at least accept, the patterns of the "consumer civilization." In the West, the same tendency on the part of the younger generation causes reaction and apprehension among many of the bourgeoisie, who are still attached to the values of the period preceding the explosion of "mass civilization." Yet the Western bourgeoisie is almost revolutionary compared to the Soviet political bureaucracy, which purely and simply lacks the conceptual elements that might enable it to understand what is taking place in the world.

When the facade of political language used by the Soviet bureaucracy is stripped away, it becomes apparent that its whole point of view of society is shaped by a few narrow preconceptions and entrenched habits. Dogmatic notions of the elders; glorification of the "Old Bolsheviks"; abuse of history; insistence on "social" art; and a moralism that stresses the reward of virtue, the punishment of evil, the joy of labor, and the wickedness of parasites: these are the elements that make up the connecting tissue between the thinking and the spoken word of bureaucracy. While these concepts are expressed in terms taken from the scoria of Marxist-Leninist revolutionary verbiage, they have come to represent the essence of rigid conservatism.

It is true that many members of the political elite in the West have similarly conservative and self-righteous convictions. But these people do not aim at molding the whole of society in their own image, reducing it to the dimension of a "single bureaucracy" (in the sense that Brzezinski uses the term). Political leaders in the West leave room for the young, the artists, the technocrats, and the rebels. By contrast, the ultra-conservative Soviet party bureaucracy clings to patterns that, despite their Marxist camouflage, date back to the Victorian age, trying to impose them on the exuberant, multiform Russian society of today, whose younger generation is now in contact with the new mass civilization, with its pastimes, its dances, its way of life, even its negative features. How can this new mass impact be offset by the patriarchal patterns and habits of a world that has completely disappeared since the advent of industrial society?

In my opinion, the lazy and superannuated bureaucracy of the Soviet Union's Communist Party, busy as it is in fighting the intellectuals, in restraining the technocrats, in warding off the attacks of the Chinese Communist Party, in coping with the "people's democracies," has neither the time nor the perspicacity to realize that the society it governs is undergoing ineluctable changes; indeed, these changes are completely beyond its imagination. Moreover, by imposing restrictions that have prevented up-to-date psychological and sociological research, the party has deprived itself of the very instruments that could help it to comprehend the evolutionary trends now gathering momentum in the society.

In sum, the Soviet political bureaucracy is "unique," but it is also static. Being "unique," it may immobilize Russia for a longer time than any other previous political elite has managed. But it is hard to conceive of inertia in human affairs. Perhaps the intellectuals and technocrats will one day find, among the masses set in motion by the impact of the new global civilization, the lever necessary to force the bureaucracy to share its power.

Immobilism and Decay

ROBERT CONQUEST

"Die Politik ist keine exakte Wissenschaft," as Bismarck once reminded the Prussian Chamber. In this area, we are in the position of having to proceed, not according to any fully established laws, but by the application of historical experience in a more intuitive way: that is, in effect, by analogy. But no analogies from the past can be wholly applicable to the Soviet situation. We are, after all, in the presence of a modern technological economy that is subject to change at a totally different sort of tempo, and with qualitatively different effects from those which characterized *politically* comparable societies in the past. Nor are analogies from the present wholly applicable either, since the Soviet political structure is critically different from that of *economically* comparable societies.

Most analyses seem to exaggerate one or the other factor. We are all familiar with recent writings about Soviet and American development in terms of "convergence"—that is, the view that there is really not much difference between the two societies in the first place, and that what difference does exist is gradually disappearing. In its crudest form, this thesis is easy enough to reject, but there is a more sophisticated and subtler version of it which, in the last analysis, amounts to much the same thing. We are told, in effect, that the "essentials" of the two societies are very similar, that while there are temporary divergences in "essentials"— often, admittedly, striking enough in a superficial way—they are not to be taken much into account by serious fellows.

On the other hand, if we concentrate purely and solely on the political, we may find ourselves implying that the only significant reality in Russia is the "Byzantine" structure of top-level politics. In saying this, I naturally do not want to urge anyone to ignore this factor. In fact, it is crucial in the sense that, as it is the only kind of "politics" that currently exists in the USSR, all immediate action must take place under its rules—even if the *final* result should be a transformation of the whole scene, politics and all.

One leading scholar has suggested to me the parallel of the French Directoire. (He would not be implying the automatic succession of a Napoleon—if Napoleon had been killed at Arcola, Sieyes might have found a soldier more amenable to civilian control.) Still, we at least can make some comparison with the third-rate, faceless collective leadership, still in the Jacobin tradition, which held power in an increasingly nondescript society when their betters had driven each other out. The differences are equally obvious.

We need more "essentials" than any such particular parallels or analogies would allow us. In the Soviet Union, we must note the nature of the economy in a physical sense: a comparatively efficient but erratically modernized industrial base, supported by an incompetent agriculture, operating in a field of modern economic forces and moving, or trying to move, at modern economic tempos. We must also examine the society, that is, the human population considered under a number of significant aspects: a peasantry more or less permanently disgruntled with its position and kept in conditions which make no economic sense; peripheral nationalities amounting to a large section of the population and continually exhibiting petty signs of a potentially serious alienation; an industrial working class which has erupted here and there in strikes and riots; a large technical intelligentsia, indispensable yet only doubtfully assimilable to orthodoxy; a literary and academic "intelligentsia of ideas," largely disaffected from current orthodoxy and including or influencing a large student class; the *ofitserstvo* (military officer corps) with its own loyalties; the managerial *khozaistvenniki*; the *apparat* (taken in its broadest sense to encompass the entire vast political "class"), with its grip on the social machinery at every level. We have here a basic political framework of highly organized bureaucracy, strong and experienced but with little "give," at present sufficient to contain the social and economic forces, and not designed to cope with the unexpected. Finally, in the sphere of active politics, a few dozen or a few hundred people wield as much social "weight" (owing to the leverage of the totalitarian structure) as is usual for whole social classes, and operate, as far as power and control are concerned, with methods comparable only to those used by past despotisms.

These are simply categories, though it should instantly be apparent how different their roles and attitudes are from those of their American or other counterparts. But the Soviet population has further, uncategorizable characteristics. In the first place, this is no generalized society. It is Russia, with all its idiosyncratic history, and the Russian periphery, with all its aspirations. And second, it is a society that has lived for fifty years under a regime which, by any standards other than its own, is an extraordinary aberration. The values and attitudes of the Communist period may not have "transformed human nature" as it was hoped they would; but they have certainly penetrated.

Nor is the *apparat* itself simply a machine for retaining power. It is a highly traditionalist body with a special set of closed ideas, a body no more amenable to certain arguments than any other institution of its type. How long can Russia afford the deadly drain of the collective farm system? But, on the other hand, how can the *apparat* ever be persuaded to abandon it?

Khrushchev was (as some of us remarked) a typical transitional ruler. He saw that there was something badly wrong with the system, and he took measures in a whole series of fields to try and find a solution. They were dramatic measures, but they were not radical. Looking back, I suppose we would now all agree that the spectacle was that of a leader grasping at a series of "bright ideas" not based on any profound analysis of the requirements and incapable, even in principle, of effecting a cure. They were symptoms rather than treatments.

The period of fever has been succeeded by one of coma, and we now have a moment—perhaps only a moment—in which we can take our eyes off the sickbed and consider more coolly the possible outcomes.

To begin with, any student of Soviet affairs must have modified considerably any Marxist or quasi-Marxist views he may originally have entertained about the effects of the economy upon politics. Stalin—refusing in this as in so many

other things to accept the limitations hitherto set by sup-
posed social, moral, or other laws—created a political mechanism powerful enough to take on and control the economic
and social forces. Now it is possible for a true autocracy of
this order to carry out basic reforms that are unpalatable to
the main body of its supporters, its ruling class—as, for example, had occurred in Tsarist Russia with the emancipation
of the serfs by Tsar Alexander II. And if Nicholas II had
backed Stolypin's land reforms to the hilt, he might have
created a fairly modern Russia. In fact, from Peter the Great
on, this has been the formula for a good deal of Russian
progress.

But today the Soviet party and state are led by men without either truly autocratic power or overwhelming prestige,
and even if they recognize the necessity of truly radical
changes, they are bound not to go beyond what is acceptable
to the primitive collective mind of the *apparat* as a whole.
Thanks to his prestige, Lenin could impose his will—though
often with some difficulty—against the general party tendency, as at Brest-Litovsk or in the adoption of the NEP,
Stalin could switch policies simply because he was the unchallenged autocrat. But it seems unlikely that the regime is any
longer capable of producing—or at least of sustaining—either
an accepted leader or a major despot. And even if it were to do
so, it is doubtful that he would be a man who would see the
necessity for radical change. Shelepin—if he is indeed a man
of comparable determination and energy, and this remains
to be seen—is more likely to be so in the style of Nicholas I
rather than of Catherine the Great.

As Professor Brzezinski so effectively shows, the present
situation is one in which there is a seepage of the gray goo
of doctrinaire bureaucracy into the top political levels, which

were hitherto partially exempt. If the final crisis of the Communist regime is to begin under the present leaders, I would expect it to come not as the result of any of their specific policies, but rather through unforeseen catastrophes with which their methods, and indeed their personalities, are not fitted to cope. They will soon have to face, in some form or other, a major dislocation which their present small-scale economies and conservation measures do not go very far to avert. The Soviet economy is *in principle* overextended. It cannot compete with the Western alliance in armaments and at the same time maintain and continually modernize the increasingly complex kind of industry that has now become necessary. Perhaps Stalin, with his single will and iron nerve, could have run an electronic-and-chemical economy in the same way that he ran a steel-and-coal one, but even that is highly doubtful. No modern-style economy has been successfully created without a high and reliable incentive system for the educated technical proletariat and the technical intelligentsia. How, then, can a Russia that is no richer than Western Europe have—even in principle—both this and rockets too? And, as techniques become more subtilized in every field, the problem increases yearly.

It will be obvious that this whole question must bedevil the relations between the Soviet ideologists, military men, and administrators in various fashions, even to the point of shaking the entire structure of the state.

Without elaborating the details of the forces concerned— and it should be noted that this is even more a crisis of ideas than of economics—we can at least see that we are faced by an economy and a society whose inextinguishable tendencies run counter to the political integument at present hemming them in, thus creating conditions of a classical Marxist pre-revolutionary situation. The current regime has learned one lesson from Khrushchev—that random reforms within the system have not done any good. But the *immobilisme* to which they have instead retreated equally provides no solution. It therefore appears inevitable that the pressures will continue to build up. The question that remains to be answered is whether the political integument will be destroyed explosively or will erode away gently.

One possible course of future political evolution might be the gradual acceptance by the leadership—however reluctantly given—of genuine elections within the party and/or the gradual transformation of the perfectly adequate constitutional *forms* of the Soviet state into reality. There have at least been suggestions made lately (for example, at the Armenian Party Congress) that voters be given a choice between two candidates in elections instead of having to approve a single list. Both candidates would still be Communists, to be sure, but it would be a beginning. There is, however, no present sign of even such progress being accepted, though change might conceivably seep in through some such loophole.

On the whole, one does not see the current leadership taking anything like adequate measures in time. Nor does one see any sign of potential successors who might. Although there have been occasions in the past when obsolete political systems have been transformed without serious trouble, these instances have been comparatively uncommon. Moreover, such an evolution has usually been possible only when plenty of time was given for the principles of change to soak into every corner of the social mind. In the USSR today, one would not expect a great deal of time to be still available.

Moreover, the blockage to the free spread of ideas, especially into the minds of the ruling party, is unprecedentedly strong —even though we should perhaps not underestimate the degree of erosion even there. But the greatest difficulty of all is a simple technical point: the machinery Stalin built is organizationally effective and ideologically disciplined to the extent that it can probably keep the political integument in being lost past the stage at which other political forms would have failed. And this implies that the pressures, when they reach a critical point, will be very high indeed. One might, of course, argue from this that an explosion, if and when it comes, would very likely be violent, but that its very violence might destroy all remnants of the present political system so quickly as to make the change almost painless.

Prediction is after all limited to the adumbration of certain general possibilities. The ones I have sketched here hinge upon an analysis of the USSR as a country where the political system is radically and dangerously inappropriate to its social and economic dynamics. This is a formula for change —change which may be sudden and catastrophic, though not necessarily so. As M. Tatu says, there are a variety of possibilities, and the outcome depends on the accidents of history.

In the meantime, at least, we can watch the operative factors. We should be prepared for surprises over the next decade and should not fall into the temptation of believing the status quo to be as stable as it may appear to the superficial glance.

Totalitarian Rule and
Social Change

✳

BORIS MEISSNER

The evolutionary trends in Soviet Russia today can be understood only if the interaction between its political system and the social reality is viewed in proper perspective. This requires greater emphasis than in the past on the analysis of the internal structure of Soviet society. In the absence of any precise definition of the several social groups and their role in society, it is impossible to answer the question raised by Zbigniew Brzezinski: namely, whether the present process of change in the Soviet system represents transformation or degeneration.

Soviet society, as the product of two radical social revolutions,[1] has a Janus face. On the one hand it is a relatively primitive industrial society that is struggling with serious problems of development. On the other hand it is a class society constituted on a totalitarian basis, exhibiting a high

---

[1] What is meant here—in addition to the October Revolution, which was primarily the work of Lenin—is Stalin's "revolution from above," which performed the function of a "substitute capitalism" and "substitute Bonapartism."

degree of social stress. The complex character of Soviet society cannot therefore be understood through study of a single model: besides the totalitarian model, which reflects the political system, models of industrial societies and of the developing countries' societies must also be relied upon. In analyzing the interaction between power structure and social structure, it is most important to project a model of totalitarian society that reflects both the static and the dynamic features of totalitarian rule.

Basic Features

All past discussions about totalitarianism have been vitiated by overemphasis on mass terror as a distinguishing feature, due to the impact of the Hitler regime and Stalinism.[2] At the same time, insufficient attention has been given to the really decisive characteristics of the autocratic-totalitarian regime. These are mainly three.[3] The first is the unrestricted autocracy of the party, which is the consequence of permanent one-party dictatorship. It is this absolute absence of any restriction on the party that constitutes the principal difference between a totalitarian and an authoritarian regime, even though today the latter is often also based on a one-party dictatorship.

[2] This holds true particularly for authors like Hannah Arendt, Carl C. Friedrich, and occasionally also Brzezinski.

[3] For a detailed exposition of the three basic elements of totalitarianism of the Soviet-Communist type, cf. B. Meissner, "Wandlungen im Herrschafts-system und Verfassungsrecht der Sowjetunion" (Changes in the Government and the Constitutional Law of the Soviet Union) in Boettcher-Lieber-Meissner, *Bilanz der Ära Chruschtschow* (A Balance Sheet of the Khrushchev Era), Stuttgart, 1966, pp. 142 ff. See also Meissner, "Party and Government Reforms," in "Russia since Khrushchev," *Survey* (London), July 1965, pp. 31 ff.

The second characteristic feature is total control from above. The Soviet control apparatus extends not only to all social organizations and institutions, but also to all mass media and other sources of public information. When total control exists, the function of terror is merely to serve as a constant reminder of the efficiency of the control apparatus. Totalitarian regimes will never give up using fear as an instrument of social manipulation—but neither do they have to depend on mass terror. Not all-encompassing terror, but the control of all functions and thought in every area of the life of society, must be regarded as the distinctive characteristic of totalitarianism.

The third feature is total planning, extending not only to the economic but also to the political and cultural sectors of society. This total planning is designed to accomplish the radical transformation of the social structure, in line with the ultimate goal set by Marxist-Leninist ideology; the "socialist society" is merely a phase of transition to a perfect "communist society." The transformation of the social structure is intended to be revolutionary in terms of its underlying ideological orientation, but it is to be realized preferably by evolutionary rather than revolutionary means. Whatever the means used by the party at any given time, the operative concept is that of *control*. So long as the party possesses the will and the power to exercise control over the autonomous social processes and forms of social spontaneity that it is promoting, the society remains subjected to totalitarian rule—whatever the given relaxation.

This conclusion by no means implies that the mere exercise of control can resolve the basic conflict within Soviet society—that is, the clash between the party's demand for supremacy in matters of ideology and organization, and the

requirements of industrial evolution. Fluctuations in the en-
forcement of social sanctions are therefore an important guide
in evaluating phases of the continuing conflict.[4] The conflict
is waged chiefly between the ruling power elite, on one side,
and the managers of the economy, together with the prestige
elite (made up mainly of writers, artists, and scientists) on
the other. The power elite consists mostly of the portion of
the "leadership cadres" that may be described as the top-level
bureaucracy (*Hochbürokratie*). The remaining portion of the
"leadership cadres" is made up of the top-level managers of
the economy, who in the main represent the technical and
economic intelligentsia. The prestige elite represents the
scientific and cultural intelligentsia, which is also referred to
as the "creative intelligentsia" (*tvorcheskaia intelligentsiia*)
in the Soviet Union.

The Intelligentsia

Consequently, what we are dealing with is not, as is so often
asserted, a single class of functionaries, making up a social
bloc of white-collar workers of a cohesive, broadly-based intelligentsia. The top-level bureaucracy, by reason of the social
functions which it performs as a result of the totalitarian
power structure—that is, functions of command and control
as well as of planning—is sharply distinguished from other
groupings that might normally be described as "white-collar."[5] Similarly, the intelligentsia—using the term in a narrow

[4] See P. Chr. Ludz, "Entwurf einer soziologischen Theorie totalität
verfasster Gesellschaft," (Sketch of a Sociological Theory of a Society
Based on Totalitarianism), in *Studien und Materialien zur Soziologie
der DDR*, Cologne-Opalden, 1964, pp. 18 ff.

[5] Cf. B. Meissner, *Sowjetgesellschaft im Wandel. Russlands Weg zur
Industriegesellschaft* (The Transformation of Soviet Society. Russia's
Way to Industrial Society), Stuttgart, 1966, p. 104.

sense to denote those people with specialties based on university or higher technical-school training—can be distinctly set off from the foremen and skilled workers with white-collar status, as well as from clerical employees. The only place where overlapping occurs is between the ruling power elite and the technical-economic intelligentsia, which virtually constitutes a supply or base group for the top-level bureaucracy. One of the decisive problems in this relationship is the fact that the top-level bureaucracy even to this day is largely made up of persons of proletarian or peasant origin, possessing an educational background inferior to that of the members of the intelligentsia. The bureaucracy also includes many so-called specialists who joined the party in the period before the war and in most cases have not had a thorough technical training.[6]

The distinction between these two controlling social groups lies primarily in the fact that the power of the top bureaucrats rests in the *positions* they hold, while that of the intelligentsia is rooted in the authority and prestige inherent in the *functions* it performs. The basis of authority as well as of prestige in modern industrial society is specialized knowledge. This is as true in the Soviet Union as in any other country— although Soviet industrial society has not yet entirely shaken off the eggshell of its developmental stage. Ability based on specialized knowledge is not, however, the only avenue to the top positions in society. Another essential requisite is the ability to get ahead; here personality, adaptation to the social norms prevailing within society, and personal connections are all important factors in the selection and promotion process,

[6] Cf. B. Lewytzkj, "Die Führungskräfte des sowjetischen Parteiapparates" (The Leadership Forces of the Soviet Party Apparatus), *Osteuropa* (Stuttgart), No. 15, 1965, pp. 739 ff.

quite aside from the question of performance.[7] The ability to get ahead is much more decisive in the hyper-bureaucratized Soviet society, with its single-party system, than in democratic industrialized societies. Contributing to the individual's success in this connection are a knowledge of ideological doctrines and power techniques, recognized service in the organization, and party patronage under the "nomenclature system."[8]

The subordination of specialized ability to the ability to get ahead, particularly in the filling of top positions, is responsible for the marked class character of Soviet society on the one hand, and the flexibility and heterogeneous nature of the ruling class on the other. From this standpoint, the democratic Western industrial societies—all their structural weaknesses notwithstanding—represent merit societies to a much higher degree than does the Soviet Union, for all its claims that the merit principle is a basic element in the organization of work.

In the Soviet Union, it is primarily those with university or higher technical-school training who possess the specialized knowledge that is needed by an industrial society in the nuclear age. Even if they do not occupy positions of power, their functions are so crucial that they can influence, at the side of those exercising actual power, the determination of the social norms and sanctions of society. Together with the leading party cadres, this merit elite is to be found mainly in

[7] Cf. O. Dreitzel, *Elitebegriff und Sozialstruktur* (Elite Concept and Social Structure), Stuttgart, 1962, pp. 100 ff.

[8] Cf. Meissner, *Sowjetgesellschaft im Wandel*, p. 103; B. Lewytzkj, "Die Nomenklatur. Ein wichtiges Instrument sowietischer Kaderpolitik (Nomenclature. An Important Instrument of Soviet Cadre Policy), *Osteuropa*, No. 11, 1961, pp. 409 ff.

the upper stratum and the upper middle stratum of society. Within this elite, special prestige attaches to scientists, writers, and artists, which permits them to exert an influence—beyond the scope of their own stratum and sometimes in opposition to the ruling group—on the practices of society as a whole.[9] The value concepts of Soviet society are in some instances more strongly shaped by the intellectual influences emanating from this prestige elite than they are by the accomplishments of the managers of the economy or the norms prescribed by the ruling power elite. This fact is clearly borne out by a sociological survey conducted by the Philosophical Institute of the USSR Academy of Sciences in 1961-62, which dealt with the values and aspirations of an elite group of Soviet youth.[10]

The top-level bureaucracy and the intelligentsia thus constitute two social groups which, irrespective of their further subdivisions, are clearly distinct in terms of their origin, their social functions, and their relationship to power.

Some Pertinent Statistics

What proportion of the working population and of the CPSU do these two groups represent?[11] In 1959 the "leading cadres," irrespective of their levels of education, and the members of

[9] Cf. the revealing report by Mihajlo Mihajlov, *Moscow Summer*, New York, Farrar Strauss, 1965.

[10] Cf. G. Wagenlehner, "Die empirische Sozialforschung in Sowjetunion" (Empirical Social Research in the Soviet Union), *Moderne Welt* (Düsseldorf), No. 6, 1965, pp. 410 ff.

[11] The sources of the figures that follow are cited in *Sowjetgesellschaft im Wandel*; in *Osteuropa*'s special issue devoted to the Twenty-third CPSU Congress; and in the author's forthcoming article, "Die soziale Struktur der KPdSU" (The Social Structure of the CPSU), *Osteuropa*, September 1966.

the intelligentsia in all areas of activity totalled 12.7 million —that is, 60 per cent of all white-collar employees. Of this total, the top-level bureaucracy (excluding the military) numbered 0.4 million, the technical and economic intelligentsia (including the industrial managers) 7 million, and the scientific and cultural intelligentsia (including the prestige elite) 5.3 million. A "ruling class" with a core of 0.4 million was thus confronted with a 12.3-million member intelligentsia, using the term in the broad sense; of these, 8 million comprised the intelligentsia in the narrower sense—specialists with university or higher technical-school education.

CPSU membership figures for 1961 indicate that party members belonging to the "leadership cadres" and the intelligentsia (in the broad sense) constituted 77.7 per cent of the 4.5 million gainfully-employed Communists in the employee category, exclusive of the military. In absolute figures, party members in the top-level bureaucracy numbered about 0.2 million (4.1 per cent); in the technical and economic intelligentsia, 2.3 million (52.1 per cent); and in the scientific and cultural intelligentsia, 1 million (21.5 per cent). In terms of overall party membership (1961: 9.3 million), these three groups represented 2.1 per cent, 24.7 per cent, and 10.7 per cent of the total. The variations in these percentages in the period up to 1966 have been minimal.

An entirely different picture emerges when these ratios are compared with the representation at the 23rd Party Congress of the CPSU and the composition of the new Central Committee.[12] The top-level bureaucracy (exclusive of the military), comprising just 2.1 per cent of the total party membership, accounted for nearly 40 per cent of the party delegates, and emerged with 81.1 per cent representation among the full

[12] Cf. this author's analysis of the 23rd CPSU Congress in *Osteuropa* and *Europa-Archiv*.

members of the Central Committee. The industrial managers and the technical and economic intelligentsia, representing about 25 per cent of the total party membership, accounted for 14.2 per cent of the Congress delegates, and only 2.1 per cent of the Central Committee members. The prestige elite and the scientific and cultural intelligentsia got a higher percentage of representation on the Central Committee than among Party Congress delegates, but this fact is not significant since—almost without exception—the authors, artists, and scientists on the Central Committee function as aides to the official cultural functionaries of the party.

While party congresses have always been shows of strength on the part of the ruling power elite, what makes the 23rd Party Congress different is its reflection of the sociological effects of the Kosygin economic reform, by which the power position of the state and economic bureaucracy has been greatly strengthened in relation to the party bureaucracy. This has restored the situation that existed prior to 1957. The industrial managers appear as only secondary beneficiaries of this development, and so far—as the Central Committee figures indicate—the reform has not increased their influence on the policy-making process. As for the prestige elite, party opposition to the expansion of its social influence was reflected in the removal of several progressive Soviet writers, among them Tvardovski and Surkov, from the Central Committee.

Thus nothing has been changed in the actual class structure of the party. The economic reform has resulted in a better balance within the top-level bureaucracy and has at the same time strengthened the position of the power elite as a whole. As the state and economic bureaucracy has gained influence, the "party organizers" within the party bureaucracy have been reduced to their control function. At the same time, the 23rd Party Congress revealed the effort of the "party ideologists," through stronger emphasis on ideological control, to preserve the primacy of the party bureaucracy and to give new confidence to the full-time party apparatus.

Whereas the party leadership is recruited without exception from the top-level bureaucracy, the intelligentsia is the key social group in the rank and file of the party. The conflict arising out of the party leadership's absolute monopoly of power is intensified by the conflict of generations resulting from the considerable age difference between the leadership and the rank and file. An age analysis of the party shows that 2.5 million members (20 per cent) today are under 30 years of age, and 4.6 million (53 per cent) are less than 40 years old. The middle generation (51 to 60 years of age) and the old generation together account for only 22.1 per cent of the total party membership, yet most of the top functionaries come from these groups. The younger generation, comprising over one-half of the party rank and file, and 47.1 per cent of the party as a whole, has no representation in the top leadership at all; this group in the main joined the CPSU in the "destalinization" period, after 1956.

In the intelligentsia, men and women are about equally represented. However, the influence women have in the leadership of the party is remarkably weak: though women, who make up 20.2 per cent of the total party, constituted 23.3 per cent of the Congress delegates, only 5 (2.6 per cent) emerged as full members of the Central Committee, and none is now included in the supreme party leadership.

Conflicts and Tensions

All of these statistics demonstrate that the gap between the top-level bureaucracy and the intelligentsia, far from diminishing, has widened in recent years. The ruling power elite is increasingly regarded as parasitic, for two reasons. In the first place, it represents a foreign body in the fabric of the elite structure of an industrialized society, since it does not submit to the economic rationality that is characteristic of an industrial merit society. The goal of promoting the conditions for existence and growth is only of secondary relevance to it. Its primary objective is the consolidation and expansion of its power base.

Second, the ruling elite is immensely exploitative of the other social groups. Through its absolute monopoly of power and unrestricted control over the means of production and property of the state, it is in a position to divert a disproportionately large share of the social product to the achievement of its political objectives, and at the same time to secure a higher personal income for its members. These advantages would be reduced if a larger proportion of the social product were to be applied to economic investment and mass consumption. As a result there is a marked conflict of interest within the "leading cadres" between the power elite and the managers of the economy, who aspire to a greater recognition of economic factors in policy-makeup and to an expansion of industrial autonomy as well as "personal property." Even deeper is the conflict of interest between the ruling elite and the prestige elite, which seeks to enlarge the sphere of individual freedom through curtailment of the omnipotence of the state.

The managers of the economy and most members of the prestige elite, in exercising their leadership functions, hold state offices. Despite this, they are much closer to the other strata of Soviet society than is the ruling power elite, whose core is the full-time party apparatus. To be sure, social tensions exist not just between rulers and subjects, but also between the intelligentsia and the popular masses; yet the latter range of tensions differs in that they are "nonantagonistic," in Marxist terms.

In evaluating the possibilities for social change under the conditions of totalitarian rule, it is irrelevant in the last analysis whether the intelligentsia (in the narrower sense) is viewed as a distinct class or whether its top group is looked upon as a counter-elite. In either event, the intelligentsia must be regarded as the force pushing the reform efforts associated with "destalinization," which are in part openly directed against the party bureaucracy as the nucleus of the "ruling class." The conflict of roles which marks the existence of the intelligentsia has, to be sure, prevented it up till now from developing that dynamic force that would have enabled Soviet society to embark upon a post-totalitarian phase of evolution.

Given the special position of all those whose role is primarily social leadership in a modern industrial society as opposed to political rulership, would it not be appropriate to conclude, as Ralf Dahrendorf, the German sociologist, has done, that the social conflict arising out of the very structure of rule constitutes the most productive source of social change, and that the social change can come only in the form of a revolutionary upheaval?[13] In the opinion of this author, this theory has much to recommend it, in that it correctly points to the constant danger posed to the rulers by a party which—as the only authorized political organization in the country—may itself become the breeding ground of revolutionary trends and movements. What it neglects to take

[13] R. Dahrendorf, "Zu einer Theorie des sozialen Konflikts" (Toward a Theory of Social Conflict), *Hamburger Jahrbuch für Wirtschafts und Gesellschaftspolitik*, vol. 3, Tübingen, 1958, p. 90.

sufficiently into account, however, are the pressures for more gradual change exerted by those who exercise functions of social leadership as opposed to political ruling functions. It is these pressures which, once set in motion, cause the gradual erosion of the autocratic-totalitarian system, thus in turn creating conditions for accelerated social change as well.

An important role in this connection is also played by conflict existing within the "ruling class," since this class includes elements which want to have rule interpreted in terms of social leadership. The power elite in the USSR is by no means the unified body it is so often believed to be. There are frictions not only between the party and state bureaucracy, but also between various sectors of the top-level bureaucracy and the mass organizations, especially labor unions, as well as between the bureaucracy and the military. The power elite includes forces, lodged for the most part in the area of the state, which oppose the power monopoly of the full-time party apparatus. The case of Colonel Penkovsky shows that this attitude also exists among high-ranking military officers.

The same disunity exists within the party bureaucracy itself where distinctions must be drawn between national, regional, and local levels of the apparatus. Stalinist opposition, in essence expressed inertia, is much more pronounced at the district and regional levels than in the central party office in Moscow or in the basic party organizations.

The conflicts which contribute to social change therefore operate horizontally as well as vertically in the power structure. Democratic societies are characterized by free competition among the groups of the elite. Such a situation does not exist in totalitarian societies; yet a limited pluralism of the elite can be noted even within the framework of autocratic-totalitarian systems.

Prospects for Change

Two consequences follow from the present situation. First, the progressive forces in Soviet society, particularly the creative intelligentsia, are making efforts to accomplish a speedy social change through reforms. "Progressive" applies to all social forces which, whether they lean more to the "liberal" or to the "conservative" side,[14] seek a decisive repudiation of totalitarianism. The principal confrontation in this connection takes place within the Soviet upper stratum, involving the top-level bureaucracy on one hand, and the university-trained group among the managers of the economy, together with progressive elements of the party elite, on the other. The upper middle stratum has not been touched by this confrontation to any great extent.

Kosygin's economic reform has brought the managers of the economy greater freedom of action. At the same time, progressive authors, artists, and scientists within the party elite have demanded a more liberal cultural policy and have courageously denounced all attempts at "restalinization." This situation has compelled the present leadership in the

[14] In this writer's opinion, the distinction drawn by Brzezinski between "leftists," "centrists," and "rightists" in the political spectrum of the USSR relies on an obsolete historical pattern. A distinction between "liberal," "conservative," and "restorative" forces would seem more apposite today. Among the "conservatives" a differentiation can again be made between "liberal conservatives," the conservative "center," and the "ultra-conservatives." The reform wing includes liberal "revisionists" and "liberal conservatives," while the orthodox wing contains both "ultraconservatives" and restorative "dogmatists." Finally, the radicals of both wings also include revolutionaries.

Kremlin, despite the ultraconservative forces still exerting pressure within its ranks, to introduce reforms which sometimes go farther than Khrushchev ever did.

On the other hand, the leadership's fear of more far-reaching experiments is unmistakable. Khrushchev's successors could soften the conflict between the ruling elite and the progressive forces among the intelligentsia only if they were prepared to curtail the permanent and absolute dictatorship of the party and emancipate large areas of social life from party control. This applies especially to the various branches of the humanities and social sciences and the area of literary and artistic creativeness. Such a development would not mean the end of Bolshevik one-party rule, but it would mean a transition from the totalitarian to an authoritarian system. The process would be comparable, for instance, to the transformation of absolutism (at a time in history when despotic features had already diminished greatly) into *enlightened* absolutism. The transformation of totalitarian rule into authoritarian rule, such as projected by the conceptions of reform communism, would be a gigantic step forward from the standpoint of Soviet society. Authoritarianism would mean a type of dictatorship that would be content with the centralization of political power, limited control over some sectors of society and a skeletal form of planning that would mainly concentrate on the economy. Whether such a development would be a step in the direction of genuine liberalization or even democratization is difficult to foresee; given the strength of Russian nationalism, for example, a form of Russian national communism might in the end adopt fascist features.

The Communist Party, using ideology and the methods of totalitarian rule, has always been successful in enforcing unity in the face of class division and in integrating divergent social groups and forces into a single body. This task is becoming increasingly difficult with the growing complexity and, in the sociological sense, greater density of Soviet society. There is a steadily growing number of people who feel that the party, in its totalitarian form, is an obstacle to the continued development of Russia, and who are working toward abolition of the exploitative features of the Soviet class society.

The Changes Ahead

JAYANTANUJA BANDYOPADHYAYA

It seems to me that the most crucial question raised by Professor Brzezinski concerns the nature of the policy alternatives confronting the Soviet leadership at the present time. If it is true, as he supposes, that there is no longer any wide divergence between possible policy alternatives in the Soviet system, then there is very little reason to expect—despite the evils of bureaucratization—any radical changes in the system as a whole, which can move forward without any great difficulty through such adaptations and adjustments as Brzezinski suggests (at least one of which was, in fact, already tried by Khrushchev). If, on the other hand, it can be shown that widely divergent policy alternatives are in fact clamoring for attention, and that many interest groups and large sections of the Soviet population would prefer policies which are radically different from those followed by the present leadership, then drastic redistributions of power and even a challenge to the Soviet political system itself cannot be regarded as improbable.

It is my contention that Professor Brzezinski underestimates the fundamental contradictions which still exist in the

Soviet system at present; and that he consequently minimizes the divergence of possible policy alternatives facing those in power. This leads him to present an oversimplified picture of the possible direction of future change and to offer suggestions for "transformation" of the system which seem to me grossly inadequate.

Marx believed that the relations of production acted as a restraint on the productive forces in a capitalist society, and that these relations, being rigid and unchangeable through evolutionary processes, could and would be upset only by revolution. Marx proved to be a false prophet, for what he called the relations of production showed a remarkable degree of elasticity in capitalist societies and changed almost beyond recognition in all their manifestations, mainly owing to the growth of political democracy and of the countervailing power of trade unions—developments which Marx regarded as impossible.

It is in the Soviet system, on the other hand, that the relations of production have proved rigid and have acted as a serious restraint on the productive forces. This "inner contradiction" of the Soviet system is most acutely manifest in the agricultural sector. Even a slight knowledge of the record of Soviet agriculture would convince anyone that collectivization has failed, that the root cause of failure has been the deadening of the collective farmer's initiative, and that the solution lies in at least a partial return to private ownership of land. But on account of the doctrinaire foundation of the Soviet state, the party has kept its eyes closed to this obvious solution and contented itself with periodically finding convenient scapegoats within the top leadership. This contradiction is present in the industrial sector also, but in less acute form since here it is possible to improve performance considerably by such measures as decentralization of decision-making and devolution of responsibility, and by relating wages to productivity and efficiency to profit—measures with which the Soviet Union has been experimenting, not without some success. So far as the industrial sector is concerned, the effect of the relations of production on the forces of production is in fact not very different in a Communist society from what it is in a capitalist society. In neither case does the worker own the factory. So long as his minimum demands are satisfied, it hardly makes any difference to him whether an industrialist or a bureaucrat is sitting on top of him. The case is obviously different with agriculture, where initiative in production clearly seems to come from the peasant's attachment to his land.[1]

In other words, I think that the contradiction between the relations of production and the forces of production in Soviet agriculture is of a fundamental nature and cannot be removed by any patchwork compromises. Moreover, I believe that the forces of liberalization which have been in operation since the death of Stalin will bring this contradiction to the surface of Soviet political life in the near future. The peasantry is likely to become more and more vocal and to find, among the younger political leaders, economists, and the Moscow-Leningrad intellectuals, advocates who will press for a reorganization of the relations of production in agriculture, involving the virtual abandonment of collective farming and a partial return to private ownership. Lenin and Stalin believed that the "commanding heights" which the

---

[1] Incidentally, the Western economists who have recently been talking of the convergence of the two economic systems ought in fact to be talking only of the two industrial systems, since there is no sign whatever of any convergence of the opposing systems of agriculture.

revolutionary leadership had to conquer were in the industrial sector; I believe that the Soviet Union will witness the
emergence in the near future of a new group of Bukharins
who will find the new commanding heights in agriculture.
Hence, when Brzezinski says that "for the moment, the era
of grand alternatives is over in the Soviet society" I think he
is clearly wrong.[2]

Another inner contradiction of contemporary Soviet society
which Professor Brzezinski, in my opinion, does not ade-
quately analyze is the contradiction between dogma and reason. Reason has crept into the minds of the Soviet people
largely, it seems to me, through the growth of scientific education. Marx and Engels, no scientists themselves, argued that
dialectics were the law of nature and that dialectical materialism as applied to human society therefore had a scientific
basis. After the revolution, political fanaticism, the intellectual regimentation of the entire population by the one-party
government, the personal tyranny of Stalin in particular, and
the relatively backward state of education among the Soviet
people all combined to push this dogma down the throats of
the Soviet intelligentsia. Thanks, however, to the phenomenal

[2] At one place toward the end of his essay, Brzezinski, in cautioning
the Soviet leadership against complacency, does make the observation
that "persistent difficulties in agriculture could some day prompt a
political aspirant to question the value of collectivization." The gap between this casual statement and the analysis I have presented above is
the measure of our disagreement.

Incidentally, Brzezinski makes an exception to his general analysis in
the case of foreign policy, where he thinks that questions of war and
peace may become the subject of a great debate in the Soviet Union in
the near future. Space does not permit me to go into this question, but
I should like merely to state my own opinion, for what it may be worth,
that this is the sphere in which a great debate is least likely.

expansion of scientific education in the Soviet Union, large sections of Soviet youth, young scientists and intellectuals, in particular, have since discovered the alleged dialectics of nature to be false, and many of them have already gathered the courage to say so, as the excellent articles in the November-December 1965 issue of *Problems of Communism* corroborated.[3] From here, it is not a long way to the realization that dialectical materialism is not a law of history either, and that the entire edifice of the Soviet state apparatus has been subsisting too long on false premises. I have no doubt that such fundamental questions have been troubling the minds of the Soviet intelligentsia and will soon find expression through young political leaders. Had there been a growth of new political institutions *pari passu* with this intellectual awakening, there would be no grounds for anticipating any radical developments in Soviet politics in the near future. Unfortunately, however, the institutional framework of the Soviet state has remained as doctrinaire and rigid as ever, in spite of its inability to satisfy the needs of the diverse new interest groups which have emerged in Soviet society. I therefore believe, unlike Professor Brzezinski, that drastic institutional changes are very likely to occur in the Soviet Union in the near future, and these changes will be facilitated by the declining hold of the party on the various interest groups. For, contrary to what Marx thought, a revolution in ideas almost always plays an autonomous and decisive role in history.

Another major shortcoming of Brzezinski's analysis, in my view, is that he treats the Soviet political system as more or

[3] This development could not possibly have taken place through the medium of the social sciences, because these are much more easily regimented than the natural sciences.

less insulated from international politics and neglects to examine the probable impact of world politics on the future evolution of the system. To begin with, the opening up of Soviet society to the radiation of Western influences, which has progressed substantially in the post-Stalin era, seems likely to be an irreversible process, especially in view of the Sino-Soviet conflict. Soviet scholars and delegations visiting Western countries in steadily increasing numbers have discovered that their own textbooks of history contain many lies. Recent years have also seen a growing appreciation among the Soviet people, especially the intelligentsia and youth, not only of Western culture but also of the political processes of the West, and this, I think, will inevitably—though perhaps imperceptibly for a while—influence the direction of political changes in the Soviet Union.

In the second place, external pressures on the Soviet leadership to refrain from acting "undemocratically" and from suppressing economic aspirations for political purposes are greater today than ever before. The fact that Communist China, which has a population of about 750 million as against the Soviet Union's 200 million, not only is determined to wrest the leadership of the Communist world from Moscow, but also has even laid claim to 84,000 square miles of Soviet territory, makes it imperative for the Soviet leadership to ensure domestic peace and a very high rate of economic and scientific development, and therefore to accept, however reluctantly, such institutional changes as seem necessary for achieving these objectives. Moreover, ever since the Soviet leadership accepted the policy of peaceful coexistence (largely as a result of the balance of nuclear deterrence and measurable economic progress at home), Moscow's foreign policy toward the Afro-Asian countries has been based primarily

on projecting an image of the Soviet state as a peaceful, democratic, prosperous, and scientifically-advanced country which
offers the "third world" a more attractive alternative than the
Western political model. The Soviet leaders, I think, will not
readily tarnish this image; and this impulse, too, seems likely
to influence their willingness to accept necessary institutional
changes.

It is not possible in this brief comment to discuss the alternative possibilities that the inner contradictions of the contemporary Soviet political system present. I agree with Professor Brzezinski that there is no possibility of the reappearance of personal tyranny, and I hope it has become clear from
the trend of my argument that I do not expect a revolution.
What I consider most likely is that within the next ten or
fifteen years a group of nonconformist leaders, approximately
belonging to the Systemic Left in Brzezinski's chart, will
come to power in the Soviet Union through the Central Committee of the CPSU; that they will accomplish this with the
support of the peasantry, the youth, and the intelligentsia in
the face of opposition from the bureaucracy, with the army
remaining more or less neutral; and that these new leaders
will initiate radical institutional changes both in the economy
(especially in agriculture) and in the political system. That
such a development is possible has, I think, been proven by
the phenomenon of Khrushchev. I hope I have also made it
clear from these comments that I see more signs of regeneration than of degeneration in current sociopolitical trends in
the Soviet Union.

The Crises Ahead

ISAAC DON LEVINE

How did the "pedestrian" Brezhnev-Kosygin team of "clerks" manage to oust the man who had outmaneuvered Stalin's cohort of Machiavellian political bosses from Malenkov to Molotov? How did these "specialists in shuffling papers and in bureaucratic procedure" pull off the overthrow of Khrushchev in an overnight operation which is the nearest thing to a coup d'etat in the entire 47-year history of the Soviet regime? Is it not tenable that behind the masks of the run-of-the-mill "clerks" lurk masters in the art of power-wielding, whose craftsmanship probably evoked the envy and admiration of the deposed leaders of the successive anti-party groups?

These were some of the questions which came to the writer's mind upon reading Zbigniew Brzezinski's stimulating analysis [which] elaborated a thesis he had launched immediately after the fall of Khrushchev in the November 14, 1964, issue of *The New Republic* under the provocative title, "Victory of the Clerks." Reading it at the time, I could not help recalling how Trotsky popularized Sukhanov's description of the early Stalin as "a grey blur" hovering in the arena of the Revolution. During the years which have elapsed since the dismissal of Khrushchev, almost nothing has cropped up in documentary form to expose the technique employed by the "clerks" in toppling the man who for a decade exercised supreme power in the Soviet Union—an achievement which certainly suggests consummate conspiratorial talents.

Professor Brzezinski's projection of the present Soviet leaders in diminutive outline against the grand personalities of their predecessors, dealing in the same dimension with the current issues as compared with the grand dilemmas the Kremlin wrestled with in bygone years, overlooks a significant factor. History has a way of enriching, glamorizing, and magnifying both the personalities and the issues marking critical turns in the life of a nation. With the passage of time, with the appearance of personal memoirs and documentary records, a national crisis takes on a depth and perspective which lift the contest for power from the level of pedestrian clashes to that of a heroic crossing of swords. In the first decade of Soviet rule, the issues that divided the leaders—such as Trotsky's proposal for the militarization of labor, the debate over "scissors" in the economy, the Bukharin-Rykov "enrich yourselves!" slogan raised for the peasantry, to cite but a few examples—lacked the luster with which they were later endowed when the rivalry for power assumed dramatic scope.

I could elaborate upon this from my personal experiences as an observer in the Soviet Union during those years, but the heart of the problem posed by Professor Brzezinski lies elsewhere, in the area of the issues confronting the Soviet system. He argues that the era of "grand alternatives," of "grand dilemmas," is for the moment over in Soviet society. I would argue that the issues which are now visibly sprouting in Soviet soil after half a century of delusional experimentation are in the process of ripening into major critical conflicts. And upon the outcome of these looming crises depends the answer to the question, "Whither Russia" in the foreseeable future.

There are at least four major divisive issues in the making that have all the earmarks of developing into decisive historical events. Of these none is more crucial or fraught with more explosive consequences than the issue of decollectivization, which has been inexorably rising before the Soviet oligarchy. The fact that the problem of Soviet agriculture has been a chronic crisis does not make it less pressing as time marches on. The contrary is true, as evidenced by the Kremlin's purchase of grain abroad in recent years at the cost of almost three billion dollars, a record-breaking figure in Soviet annals. This unprecedented expenditure makes the issue even more pressing in view of the drain it puts upon the dwindling gold reserves of the country. Stalin's system of collective farming has proven itself a dismal failure, and its modernization for another lease on life would require immense capital investments far beyond the capacity of the Soviet state.

Without eventual decollectivization, it is becoming evident, the Soviet Union will be unable to raise enough food for its increasing population and to produce the commodities which are indispensable to the development of modern industry. The best and latest studies on Soviet agriculture, which on a per capita basis has barely caught up with the 1913 level of production, leave little doubt that a grave internal crisis is brewing for the ruling elite on the collectivization front. But there is also little doubt that the gravity of the challenge of decollectivization cannot fail to create a gulf within the collective leadership, as the inevitable lag in Soviet agriculture becomes more and more pronounced.

Grave, too, is the second grand dilemma which is already bedeviling the Moscow elite—the growing backwardness in the organization of production and consumption of goods, arising from the widening gap between ever-advancing technology and the obsolete Marxian economic system. The victory of Communist economics was predicted by Lenin and his successors upon their becoming more efficient than the economics of capitalism. As succinctly summed up by C. Olgin of the Munich Institute for the Study of the USSR, in a conference sponsored by the Royal Institute of International Affairs in London, performance "is impossible without the free circulation of socio-economic as well as technical and scientific information."[1] The problem of the truly phenomenal inefficiency and wastefulness of the Soviet economy has grown more glaring and urgent with the advent of the era of automation and the galloping efficiency of the foremost capitalist economies. No longer is the challenge one of catching up and surpassing the productive and distributive systems of the United States, Germany, or Japan. Nor is the challenge one which can be met by the rise of a new caste of technicians, engineers, and scientists, as some have contended who see in that caste an alternative to the old-line political leadership. When an engineer is installed in political office, he ceases to be an engineer.

Rather, the challenge before the Kremlin is how long the stranglehold of totalitarian repression can continue to choke off the flow of free inquiry trickling into the Soviet state organization from the highly advanced capitalist nations,

[1] See *Bulletin* (Munich), published by the Institute for the Study of the USSR, April 1966.

from the pressures of the new technological caste, and from political destalinization, which is spawning a generation that has lost both interest and faith in the creed of Marxism-Leninism. Without the religious anchors of that creed, the Soviet ship of state is bound to drift on an uncharted sea, creating division in the commanding echelon. How long will it be before the attempt of Mihajlo Mihajlov to establish a second political party with an opposition press in Yugoslavia is emulated in the Soviet Union? As in the case of the issue of decollectivization, this second challenge of what might be called Menshevization raises a Gargantuan problem for the high priests of the Lenin cult.

So much for the divisive issues on the home front. In the realm of foreign affairs, Professor Brzezinski reluctantly concedes, "one can perhaps argue that grand dilemmas still impose themselves on the Soviet political scene." What an understatement of the overwhelming dilemma confronting the Kremlin as a result of the challenge of an aggressive and jingoistic Maoist China! It has been manifest since the outbreak of the Indian-Chinese armed conflict in 1960 that the general staff of the Soviet Army, backed by the party elite, threw its support to India against Red China because of the latter's territorial claims against the Soviet Union. These claims, when one includes Outer Mongolia, cover an area of over two million square miles, more than a quarter of the Soviet land mass.

The considerations of national security which dictated the policy of Soviet aid to India were also responsible for the Kremlin's launching of a "good neighbor" diplomacy along the entire tier of states lying to the south of China and on her flanks, from Pakistan and Afghanistan to Iran and Turkey. The stationing of some 17 Soviet divisions on the 6,000-mile border separating the two Communist powers, the creation of an armed buffer zone along the Sinkiang-Kazakhstan frontier, where thousands of shooting affrays have admittedly occurred, the extraordinary attention bestowed by Moscow's supreme rulers upon their Outer Mongolian vassals—all these things testify to a festering crisis over vital national interests between China and Russia. Perhaps nothing symbolizes the profound tension in their relations so much as the demolition in Peking by Mao's Red Guards of the monument to Pushkin, Russia's national poet and the pride and glory of all her people. It is not to be expected that Peking would throw down the gauntlet to Moscow on the field of battle. But it would be shortsighted to disregard the lesson of history that an arms race carries within it the seeds of conflict, and this race in itself presents the Kremlin with a divisive issue of the first magnitude.

Hand in hand with Communist China's challenge is the threat of the nuclear rearmament of Germany, which is emerging as still another major issue confronting Moscow with ever-growing urgency. Western leaders are at last realizing that West Germany's pressure to become a full nuclear power is regarded in the Soviet Union as a reappearance of the sword of Damocles which hung over them so long. This is a psychological condition which no rationalization of the exact role assigned to Germany under NATO control can dispel. The Russian fear that a resurgent Germany may seize the keys to the nuclear armories of NATO cannot be overcome by arguments. Bonn's campaign to achieve full partnership with the United States in the nuclear field signifies to the Kremlin the approach of a day when American forces will be withdrawn from Europe and West Germany will take over the role of the protagonist of European defense. In the face of such a potential threat, it is probable that the Kremlin leadership is already giving serious consideration to alternatives of the gravest possible character.

In sum, two specters are haunting the Soviet world: the specter of a domestic economy moving toward bankruptcy on the organizational and ideological fronts; and the specter of foreign threats stemming from resurgent militant nationalisms. Any one or any combination of the four grand dilemmas outlined above could well bring the present Soviet leadership to a critical crossroads within a matter of years, precipitating a struggle for power among the oligarchs. There is very little in the ferment which has wracked Soviet society in recent times to warrant the belief that a popular upheaval is in the offing, just as there is little in the past history of the country to justify the wishful thought that democratization can be achieved by reform to the point where the dictatorship will abdicate its absolutist rule.

The path of the coming change is indicated in the pattern of the coup carried out by Khrushchev in the summer of 1957 with the aid of Marshal Zhukov. That technique was improved upon by the Brezhnev-Kosygin team in the "palace revolution" of October 1964 which toppled Khrushchev. In the light of the emergence during the last three decades of an essentially nationalist Russia from the cocoon of Messianic internationalism, it is more than likely that the next phase in the transformation of the leadership will be a classical coup d'etat by a coterie of iconoclastic arch-nationalists inside the Kremlin. Such a group would discard some more of the relics of the Communist ideology and attempt to find a way out of the economic blind alley and the foreign relations impasse in which the Soviet state is now trapped.

Beyond Libermanism

※

ERNST HALPERIN

One of the symptoms of the decline in the quality of Soviet leadership so ably described in Professor Brzezinski's essay on the essential evolutionary processes of the Soviet Union is the current leaders' failure to provide adequate ideological guidance. "Ideological semantics" are not enough. What is needed is the ability to manipulate ideology, to twist and reinterpret it in accordance with the changing needs of the Soviet state. In a movement so dependent on ideological cohesion as communism, in which every important measure and every change of policy call for elaborate ideological justification, this faculty is of vital importance. Lenin and Stalin both possessed it. But Khrushchev's efforts were of indifferent quality.[1] In the later years of Khrushchev's rule, the

[1] The revisions of Leninist doctrine proclaimed at the 20th CPSU Congress were courageous and well-reasoned, but they may well have been a collective effort. Judging by his speech at the Congress, Mikoyan at least appears to have had some part in working them out. But such important Khrushchevian innovations as the abolition of machine-tractor stations and the decentralization of economic administration were introduced without any serious attempt at ideological justification. As for the new Party Program, it has always seemed to this writer, at least, to be a singularly uninspired and uninspiring document.

care of ideology came more and more to be separated from the top leadership functions and to be entrusted to personalities of the second or third rank, like the arid dogmatist Suslov, the bureaucratic pedants Pospelov and Ponomarev, and that platitudinously loquacious Polonius-figure, the late O. V. Kuusinen.

As for the present regime, neither Brezhnev nor Kosygin appears to be at all interested in ideology. Unfortunately for them, ideology cannot safely be neglected in a party and state so firmly based on ideological foundations. In such a party and state, disregard of ideology does not make it become unimportant, but merely makes it change its function: it ceases to be a dynamic force spurring the masses, or at least the cadres, to fulfill the tasks set by their leaders, and instead becomes an obstacle to progress, an invincible weapon in the hands of vested interests resisting change.

The stagnation of Soviet agriculture, for instance, can be overcome only by a basic structural reform. The ideological obstacle to such a reform is the official dogma according to which the *kolkhoz*—the collective farm—is a basic pillar of the Soviet social system. In order to overcome this obstacle it would be necessary to carry destalinization to its logical conclusion by condemning forced collectivization, by rehabilitating Bukharin politically as well as personally, and by returning to Lenin's formula of 1923: "Cooperatives plus Soviets equal socialism"—in which the word "cooperatives" signified ordinary cooperatives of the Scandinavian type. Instead of this, the Soviet leaders are reinforcing the ideological bulwarks of the present system by their partial rehabilitation of Stalin.

In industry and trade, Soviet state interest also calls for reform, while the special interests of the bureaucracy militate against it. The present regime has inherited from Stalin a rigidly centralized command economy that was hardly shaken by Khrushchev's reforms and that has proved incapable of fulfilling the demands of a modern industrialized society. The only remedy would be to transfer the operative decisions from the state bureaucracy to the managers of individual enterprises—that is, to revert to market mechanisms. That is the essence of Professor Liberman's proposals, and the encouragement of his "experiment" by the Soviet leaders shows that they are indeed aware that this would be the correct solution.

Unfortunately, "Libermanism" has one fatal flaw: it is incompatible with the Stalinist concept of socialism still viewed as the only correct outlook by the party. In this concept, the means of production are owned by society as a whole, and administered in the interests of the whole by its representative, the state. There is no room in this scheme for independent management of the individual enterprise. In whose name is the enterprise to be managed? Whom does the manager represent? How can he justify a decision taken in the interests of the enterprise, if this decision is criticized as harmful to the interests of the community by state or party bureaucrats or by the managers of rival enterprises? These and similar objections are unanswerable within the framework of Communist orthodoxy.

In the non-Communist world, the principle of private property provides ideological justification for the independent operation of the individual enterprise. Never mind that in practice, private ownership of the enterprise is frequently so diluted as to become anonymous, and that the owners have little or no control over the management. What is important is that the *principle* of private ownership justifies the independent operation of the enterprise.

But private ownership is not the only possible ideological justification for the market economy and the independence of enterprises. Cooperative ownership—that is, the collective ownership of an enterprise by its workers (or by its customers)—also provides adequate justification. A closely related concept provides the ideological base for the market economy of Communist Yugoslavia, where formally there is still social ownership of the means of production. But their use and exploitation are entrusted to the workers of the individual enterprise. Actually, the power of the organs of self-management, the Workers' Assemblies, and Workers' Councils, is limited, and they do not seriously restrict the manager's freedom of decision, although he is nominally their employee. But these organs *do* provide an adequate ideological justification for the independence of the enterprise, and thus for what is, despite much governmental interference, an authentic market-economy. Perhaps one has to live for some time in both Yugoslavia and one of the countries which have the Soviet type of command economy in order to grasp the basic difference and the superiority of the Yugoslav system.

It is highly instructive to compare the propagandistic techniques employed by the Yugoslav leaders in introducing the new system with those of the Soviet leaders in sponsoring "Libermanism."

The Yugoslav system was introduced in 1950 with a great flourishing of ideological trumpets. In his speech announcing the Law on Workers' Self-Management, Tito not only declared that he was fulfilling the old demand of the workers' movement, "the factories to the workers!" but also even went so far as to claim that the introduction of the new system was the first step toward the "withering away of the state" envisaged by Marx, Engels, and Lenin, but deliberately sabotaged by Stalin.[2] A drastic reorganization of the economy—spelling loss of employment and severe temporary hardship for many thousands of bureaucrats—was thus made to appear as an important step toward the final goal, and thereby turned into a source of ideological fervor and enthusiasm.

The Soviet leaders, on the other hand, seem to be quite deliberately downplaying the significance of "Libermanism" by presenting it as a mere practical experiment in new organizational techniques, a matter of no theoretical or ideological importance. And, while increasing the number of enterprises involved in the experiment, they are at the same time appeasing the bureaucracy by reversing the partial decentralization of economic administration implemented by Khrushchev, thus allowing numerous bureaucrats to return from their places of banishment in the provinces to the newly created ministries in the capital. It is not very likely that bureaucratic resistance to the general implementation of "Libermanism" can be overcome by such timid procedures.[3]

[2] Tito's speech in *Borba* (Belgrade), June 27, 1950. For a brief outline of the Yugoslav system and a discussion of its relevance to the problem of economic reform in the Soviet Union, see the present writer's "Revisionism and Yugoslavia" in the volume *Polycentrism* (edited by Walter Lacqueur and Leopold Labedz, New York, Praeger, 1963), and also my book, *Triumphant Heretic* (London-Toronto, Heinemann, 1958).

[3] In his illuminating report, "Soviet Reforms: The Debate Goes On" (*Problems of Communism*, January-February 1966), Michel Tatu lists the numerous obstacles impeding the implementation of the Liberman reform.

It is of course possible that the Soviet leaders will still make up their minds to give the Liberman experiment an appropriate ideological foundation by proclaiming it to signify a new and higher stage in the advance from socialism to communism, and by instituting some semblance of "workers' control" in the factories. In doing so they would not necessarily have to copy the Yugoslav pattern of Workers' Assemblies and Workers' Councils; instead, formal responsibility for the enterprise might be handed over to its trade-union organization or even to its party branch as the representative of the workers. At present, however, there is no indication that the Soviet leaders are even remotely considering such a course. On the contrary, in industry as in agriculture, the partial rehabilitation of Stalin is making it more difficult to provide ideological motivations for the urgently needed practical reforms.

In the absence of any ideological stimulus, the Liberman reform would thus appear doomed to failure—for the same reason that two successive attempts at decentralization, conducted in an equally unimaginative, unideological, and purely pragmatic manner, have already failed in Czechoslovakia.[4] In this event, a further decline in productivity and growth rate, with detrimental effects on the world-power status of the USSR, could hardly be avoided.

[4] The resistance of the Czechoslovak party and state bureaucracy to decentralization is described by J. M. Montias in "Economic Reform in Perspective," *Survey* (London), April 1966.

Evolution and Detente

✳

JOSEPH CLARK

Perhaps the most significant aspect of Professor Brzezinski's inquiry about the possible evolution of the Soviet Union "into a more pluralistic and institutionalized system" is the fact that he poses this rather optimistic possibility at all.

For a long time it was almost an article of faith that evolution toward relaxation and attenuation of totalitarianism in a Communist society was impossible. Even the revised edition of *Totalitarian Dictatorship and Autocracy*, by Brzezinski and Carl Friedrich, concludes with a rather dubious view of the chances of such evolutionary progress. Answering the question, "What then is going to be the course of totalitarian development?" the authors suggest:

If one extrapolates from the past course of evolution, it seems most likely that the totalitarian dictatorships will oscillate between an extreme of totalitarian violence and an opposite extreme of an actual breakdown.[1]

The alternatives Professor Brzezinski suggests in the present discussion are rather more in harmony with actual trends

[1] Carl J. Friedrich and Zbigniew Brzezinski, *Totalitarian Dictatorship and Autocracy*, New York, Praeger, 1965, p. 375.

in the Soviet Union. These alternatives are either "the progressive transformation of the bureaucratic and institutionalized system"—or degeneration. The very real danger of the latter is vividly illustrated by Brzezinski's apt comparison:

Indeed, the effort to maintain a doctrinaire dictatorship over an increasingly modern and industrial society has already contributed to a reopening of the gap that existed in prerevolutionary Russia between the political system and the society, thereby posing the threat of the degeneration of the Soviet system.

The turning point of Soviet evolution came in 1956. That is when the alternatives between progressive transformation or degeneration might first have been discerned. The year 1956 looms as big as 1917 for the future of communism. Without even intending it that way, Khrushchev opened up for consideration and debate the very fundamentals of communism. He did this after Stalin had, for nearly three decades, totally eliminated all debates, all disputing, all consideration of any ideas, no matter how remotely associated with politics.[2]

Khrushchev's "revelations" and the upheavals in the Communist world in 1956 inaugurated a crisis more profound than any previously experienced by communism. As in the past, the crisis posed no threat of revolution; more than ever before, however, it opened up the chance of an evolutionary development along the lines of the first possibility indicated by Brzezinski.

Each of the previous crises of communism had been surmounted: initially with a move toward total dictatorship;

[2] Writing in *Foreign Affairs*, October 1957, Isaiah Berlin observed that the greatest threat to despotic regimes comes from "discussion of ideas—disputes about issues apparently remote from politics, such as metaphysics or logic or aesthetics."

later with its intensification. Among these earlier milestones, there was the crisis of the years 1919-22, when the expectations of world revolution, at least of the German revolution, were shattered. There was the crisis of the succession after Lenin died, when the brilliant corevolutionists of Lenin were maneuvered out of power (and ultimately out of existence) by Stalin. There was the crisis of the "second revolution," when up to ten million peasants were "liquidated" (mainly because they had been the most efficient farmers in the country), and when the industrialization of Russia was undertaken by a primitive accumulation of capital squeezed from the toil of the working people. Then there was the crisis when Stalin's alliance with Hitler opened the Soviet Union to the most terrible invasion of its history, under conditions where Stalin's abject appeasement of Hitler had weakened Russia, causing it to be caught unprepared, with its planes on the ground near the border, with its troops sending sad messages to headquarters, inquiring: "We have been fired upon, what shall we do"?[3]

Why might the current crisis of communism be more difficult to surmount than the previous ones? One hypothesis holds that it is a deeper crisis because, paradoxically, it originated from the amelioration and improvement of Soviet society. Above all, there was the relaxation of terror after Stalin died. Naked police-state rule and the ubiquitous concentration camps were no longer the major institutions for maintaining Soviet power; though no institutional safeguards against the return of the terror were established, the self-interest of the new rulers, whether Malenkov, Khrushchev,

[3] John Erickson, *The Soviet High Command*, New York, St. Martin's Press, 1962, p. 587.

Brezhnev, or Kosygin, militated against a drastic reversion to terroristic methods. There was also a slow but discernible improvement of living standards which produced an expectable result—with eating came the appetite for better eating.

With the thaw came the ferment among students, intellectuals, scientists, youth. Perhaps the most incredible example of the change was the appearance of Alexander Solzhenitsyn's *One Day in the Life of Ivan Denisovich*. Not only did Solzhenitsyn write this moving story of the concentration camps, but he lived to write more—and in the great tradition of Russian humanist literature.

There was a view, widely held in the West after the 1956 upheavals, that the improvement in Soviet society could only lead to the strengthening of communism and its continued development along totalitarian lines. Reinforcing this attitude was a belief that the postwar expansion of communism to other lands, especially China, would strengthen Moscow's control and help it overcome the crisis of 1956. This appeared to leave only one bleak prospect for ever achieving surcease from the spread of communism—a nuclear armageddon.

But the "unshakable unity" of the Moscow-Peking axis proved to be something even less than figments of fears and myths. The very extension of communism (through an indigenous revolution) multiplied the problems of the Communist world, just as the improvement in Soviet life created greater demands for institutional guarantees of legality and progress. Nevertheless, the myth of a single world Communist conspiracy died slowly. The concept of a bipolar world persisted even after the Communist nations were torn apart by one of the greatest schisms in the history of nations, religions, or races—the Sino-Soviet conflict.

The year 1956 ushered in the beginning of the end of

ideology in the Soviet Union and Eastern Europe. It was Khrushchev who reminded the Communists in the satellite nations that ideology puts no goulash on the workingman's table. He might have added that neither does it assure the successful cultivation of corn on the Russian steppes.

Stalin's police-state rule stifled initiative, hindered the germination of new ideas, prevented the development of talented leadership. Stalin's iron curtain was erected as protection against the most dangerous contamination of all—ideas, dangerous thoughts that might come from contacts abroad. Just after Stalin died, an American Communist representative in Moscow attempted to convey condolences to a representative of the American Department of the CPSU Central Committee. The Soviet Communist smiled in a manner most inappropriate to the period of mourning and said: "Life goes on." Then he added: "It would be a good idea, don't you think, if we opened our doors a bit more widely, and invited even members of the American Congress to visit us." Within a short while the curtain was raised a little—for after all, it was Communist Russia that was being stifled and degraded by the curtain.

Certainly one factor that would work toward the first alternative suggested by Professor Brzezinski, the transformation of Soviet society, is the opening up of wider contacts with the Communist countries. In this respect it is puzzling to see how fearful many in the West have been of greater trade, cultural and tourist exchanges, and contacts between East and West. Basically, it has been the Communists, even after 1956, who have hindered a truly large-scale development of East-West relations. Yet, little imagination has been used to make it more difficult for them to maintain the closed doors; and certainly the West has in many instances been a reluctant dragon about developing trade with Communist lands.

There is a strange irony about the present moment in history. Communism faces its most profound crisis since the coup of 1917. Yet the West seems singularly incapable of taking advantage of this crisis. The key to the puzzle appears in another recent and perceptive study by Professor Brzezinski, where he writes:

Only in a relaxed international atmosphere could the hidden tensions and contradictions that plague the East surface and become politically important. The Communist regimes, more than the pluralistic West, require hostility and tension to maintain their unity. It is impossible to think of the Hungarian revolution or the Polish October without "the spirit of Geneva" which created a climate of relaxation; it is likewise impossible to consider the Rumanian self-assertion of 1964 occurring in the context of the war-threatening Berlin crisis. Detente inevitably challenges Soviet control over Eastern Europe.[4]

Detente also challenges the conservatism of the Communist regimes which cling to the autocracy of the past. Obviously, detente is made more difficult by the war in Vietnam. If any regime requires "hostility and tension," it is the Chinese Communist oligarchy. That regime is so much in need of hostility and tension that it would undoubtedly turn down an invitation to join the United Nations. This raises the question why Western policy is in fact catering to Communist China's desires. Why facilitate and strengthen Red China's hand by providing the tension and hostility she so urgently craves? And why make it more difficult for those

[4] Zbigniew Brzezinski, *Alternative to Partition*, New York, McGraw-Hill, 1965, p. 121.

forces in the Soviet Union which would move toward a more pluralistic and institutionalized evolution if efforts to secure detente were more actively prosecuted both in the Far East and in Europe?

The USSR and Eastern Europe

※

ALEXANDER BREGMAN

Since this discussion has focused on the nature and prospects of the Soviet political system, it is perhaps natural that the authors taking part have almost completely abstained from discussing the future of communism in the East European countries. Yet, developments in the "people's democracies" could, and probably will, affect to a considerable degree the course of events in the Soviet Union.

To be sure, changes within Russia itself are bound to generate a greater impact on the situation in the East European countries than vice versa. If, as suggested by Professor Brzezinski, reforms leading to a profound transformation of the Soviet system were to be forced upon the ruling bureaucracy in the USSR, then the other Communist bureaucracies could hardly resist pressures for similar changes; and any kind of violent upheaval in the center of the Communist world would reverberate to its periphery. In the reverse direction, the momentum would be much weaker. One can visualize a radical change in Czechoslovakia, for example—even to the extent of the emergence of a two-party system—without Moscow automatically following suit.

Nevertheless, the political and economic links between the Communist countries have by now created a kind of interdependence which makes it impossible to isolate events in any one of them. This has been so for quite some time. As early as 1956, the gains of Polish intellectuals in the wake of the "October" events had a decisive effect on the morale of the Soviet intelligentsia. The Moscow hotels were besieged by crowds of Russians anxious to buy the few Polish newspapers and journals that were available, and knowledge of Polish soon became *de rigeur* for those who thirsted for information and ideas relatively free from the stifling shackles of *Agitprop*. Today the Polish journals are no longer exceptional; Czechoslovak literary reviews are often more outspoken. Even so, the Soviet authorities decided to ban certain Polish publications, including the weekly illustrated *Przekroj* and two film reviews, on the grounds that they were disseminating "decadent" Western views.[1]

If—however improbable it may appear today—another revolution were to break out in Eastern Europe, the Soviet leaders would be faced with an even more agonizing choice than that which confronted them during the Hungarian revolution of 1956, and their course of action would undoubtedly have a profound effect in the Soviet Union itself; a lack of intervention would encourage any latent opposition, while repression might well provoke a deep feeling of solidarity with the victims.

Thus, one can hardly answer the question "whither Russia?" without also trying to determine "whither Eastern Europe?"

In view of the growing differences between the Commu-

[1] This ban went into effect on Jan. 1, 1967, according to the Moscow correspondent of *Le Monde* (Paris).

nist countries, general conjecture on the latter issue is not easy. Still, there are sufficient common features to warrant a few tentative hypotheses on the future of the present political system in Eastern Europe.

The same forces for change that have been at work in the Soviet Union are appearing all over Eastern Europe—though stronger in some countries, weaker in others. Everything Professor Brzezinski has said about the degeneration of the Soviet political system into a rigid bureaucracy "inimical to talent and hostile to political innovation" applies to the East European Communist states as well. The bureaucracies, in trying to defend their vested interests, have had to cope with the assertiveness of the technocrats, the younger generation and the intellectuals, as well as with the demands of the masses at large for more consumer goods. The party leaders are finding it difficult, especially in the more advanced states with sophisticated economies, to adapt the system to the needs of a modern society, but they remain extremely reluctant to share power with anyone.

There are also parallels to the Soviet situation with respect to the recent curb on destalinization, the halt in the liberalization process, and the adoption of harsher methods toward intellectual dissidents and other rebels, especially in Poland and Hungary.

Yet, while the similarities between the Soviet Union and the European Communist states are understandably great, the differences remain considerable. In particular, the pressures for change are greater in Eastern Europe.

The Soviet apparatus is now 50 years old. The Communist structures in the "people's democracies" are much younger—little more than 20 years on the average. In all of the countries except Yugoslavia, the Communists gained power not through domestic revolution, as in Russia, but through force imposed from without. Thus the bureaucracies are less strongly entrenched and less capable of resisting pressures; they must strive to replace rule based on force by rule based on popular consent—and they are still very far from achieving this aim.

Many other factors contribute to making the Communist system weaker in East Europe than in the Soviet Union itself. For one thing, traditions of freedom and multiparty rule are much stronger in the European countries. While some of the countries could hardly claim to have had democratic systems before the war, all have traditions of political freedom that have no match in Russian history. Moreover, all of them feel that they belong to Western civilization, and they long to rejoin Europe in spirit. Despite disappointments with Western policy on the part of the people (for instance, during the Hungarian revolution), and a considerable distrust of present Western motives on the part of the regimes, there is great admiration for the Western way of life. The desire to enjoy the benefits of "consumer civilization"—which even in the USSR shapes the attitudes of millions of people (as Mr. Galli pointed out in an earlier commentary)—is far more widespread in Eastern Europe. While Soviet citizens, comparing present conditions with those of 20 or 30 years ago, can find them greatly improved, the comparison is apt to be far less favorable for middle-aged Poles, Czechs, or Hungarians.

In addition, some Soviet citizens can find consolation for shortcomings and for the slow improvement of their everyday life in the spectacular accomplishments of the Soviet Union. While it is true that the average Soviet citizen would opt for another pair of shoes rather than for yet another

"Sputnik," there are those whose enthusiasm for the successes of their country—for example, in the conquest of space—may tend to help them forget the shortage of consumer goods. In the people's democracies there are no similar achievements for the rulers to exploit, and whatever gains have been made are generally viewed by the masses as having been won by themselves, *despite* rather than because of the Communist system of rule.

Knowledge of life in the West is also much greater in Eastern Europe. The European Communist rulers have never succeeded in cutting off their people from contacts with the West as completely as the Soviet masses were isolated up until a few years ago. Even in the years of Stalinist terror, when the Iron Curtain seemed almost impenetrable, contact was maintained, especially through radio service. Western nations have always had many times more East European than Soviet listeners. And now there are other links. Traveling to the West has become possible for a large number of people, especially Poles and Hungarians. In 1965, 150,000 Hungarians—or 1.5 per cent of the total population—visited Western countries, although stricter regulations reduced the number of travelers by some 10 to 15 per cent in 1966. By contrast, the Soviet Union, with a vastly larger population, allows only a few tens of thousands to travel to the West annually, and most of these are officials. For Czechs, Rumanians, and Bulgarians, traveling to the West remains difficult, but they are increasingly in touch with Westerners thanks to the large number of tourists visiting their countries. More important, all the East European peoples have greater access than their Soviet brothers to Western literature, art, films, music, and other cultural influences. Even women's fashions show the strong influence of French and Italian trends.

Another important factor differentiates the Soviet from the East European situation. While, of course, no organized opposition exists in any Communist country, in Eastern Europe there are strong forces which are resistive to the Communist ideology, particularly the Catholic Church. In Poland, and to a lesser degree in Hungary and Czechoslovakia, the ties of religion seriously weaken the hold of the party over the nation.

Finally, nationalism plays a quite different role in the people's democracies than in the Soviet Union. For the Soviet ruling class, the ethnic loyalties of the non-Russian nationalities constitute a problem which, as Professor Brzezinski has pointed out, may become more acute, but at least the Russian half of the population does not oppose the existing system for nationalistic reasons. On the contrary, the ruling bureaucracy is able to exploit Russian patriotism; it can make the Russians feel that, right or wrong, it is their country and their government.

In Eastern Europe nationalism could also be exploited to strengthen the Communist dictatorships; in fact, the Rumanian leadership has been doing just this with some success. By defending national interests against the Soviet Union, particularly in the economic field, by taking an increasingly independent line in international affairs, by exalting the nation's past, and by going so far as to hint that it will reclaim the territories annexed by the Soviet Union, the Ceausescu regime has gained—at least for the time being—a certain popularity that helps it resist demands for greater freedom and strengthens its hold over the nation. But the other East European regimes are either unwilling or unable to follow this example. They feel too dependent upon the Soviet Union for their survival to take the risks involved in playing up nationalist, anti-Russian feelings. Nationalism for them is a source of weakness, not of strength. They are faced with demands not only for reforms and greater freedom but also for more independence from Russia, and they continue to to be regarded as tools of Moscow.

With so many factors contributing to the weakening of the political system in most of the countries of Eastern Europe, one might be tempted to call the situation pre-revolutionary. Yet in fact it is not; the mood of the people is antirevolutionary. The nations of Eastern Europe want change, but they hope it will come about in an evolutionary way.

There are quite a few reasons for this mood, but the most important is a sense of the futility of violent revolt, as shown by the Hungarian revolution of 1956 and the East German rising of 1953, and a decade earlier by the tragic Warsaw rising of 1944. Nobody came to the aid of the insurgents; their sacrifices were in vain. These memories die hard.

Yet, while there is no indication of a revolutionary trend anywhere in Eastern Europe, it would be rash to conclude that a violent upheaval is out of the question. As Mr. Lyons rightly stressed in his commentary, revolution has always seemed "impossible" and apocalyptic until it occurred. To the examples he quoted, one could add others. Thus the bloody events in Poznan in June 1956, which paved the way for the October upheaval and which could easily have resulted in a full-scale uprising, started with a peaceful demonstration in which the participants had no thought of violence. Rebellions do not require an organization, or lead-ers, or a revolutionary plot. In the Poznan case, the error of a frightened security officer in ordering his men to open fire on an unarmed crowd in a few moments transformed a peaceful protest into a violent riot.

Several factors may in the future combine to create a climate more favorable to upheaval. First, a younger generation is coming along which has no personal memory of the uprising that failed. Young Poles were not yet born when the Warsaw uprising took place. In a few years East German and Hungarian youths will know of their elders' revolt only from hearsay. Within the last year or two the authorities in several East European countries have announced the discovery of anti-state "conspiracies," mostly involving schoolboys. Such plots might be dismissed as infantile, but they allow conjecture that the mood of apathy that has marked the last decade may be slowly passing.

Another subtle psychological change can be noticed in current evaluation of the events of 1956. Until recently the opinion prevailed that the Hungarian revolution had been totally in vain, but that the Poles, by stopping short of revolt and by being satisfied with reforms and liberalization, had gained much without any sacrifice. Yet, over a period of time Kadar has been forced to make far-reaching concessions in order to gain support and to erase the memories of his treason, while Gomulka has been busy withdrawing the concessions the party made in 1956. By now, quite a few Poles have come to think of the "Polish October" as a gigantic fraud perpetrated with great skill by the party to save itself. Although this view seems much exaggerated to the writer, the fact remains that there is little chance of a second "October." If there is another revolt, the Poles will not stop at half-measures. More important, many Poles have ceased to believe that the regime can really evolve peacefully into something better.

A third factor worth mentioning is the emergence of revolutionary groups that call on the working class to revolt against the Communist bureaucracy. Paradoxically, it is not the enemies of communism who openly advocate a revolution, but young Marxist intellectuals such as the Polish University lecturers Jacek Kuron and Karol Modzelewski, who have been in prison since 1956. In a recent open letter addressed to the Polish party and smuggled to the West for publication, they declared that "in view of the impossibility of solving the economic and social crisis within the bureaucratic system, a revolution is inevitable." In their view, the "industrialized bureaucratic states"—the USSR, Czechoslovakia, the German Democratic Republic, and Hungary—are all ripe for revolution, and while no one can forecast where a revolt may break out, there is no shred of doubt that it will spread to the whole camp.[2] While there are probably not many Marxist intellectuals of this persuasion, the fact that such trends exist among disillusioned Communists must be noted.

Perhaps the most important of the factors which make a violent change possible, even if improbable, is the view that the risk of Soviet intervention has lessened considerably since the crushing of Hungary in 1956. The fear of such intervention, which for many years was considered a virtual certainty in the event of an outbreak, has been the biggest deterrent to revolt even where discontent was extreme. Now opinion

[2] Jacek Kuron and Karol Modzelewski, *List Otwarty* (Open Letter), addressed to the Basic Party organization of the Polish United Workers' Party at Warsaw University; published under separate cover by the Paris monthly, *Kultura*, in 1966.

seems to be shifting. Certainly few East Europeans would share the conviction of Kuron and Modzelewski that Soviet intervention is already highly improbable. Since the two writers are persuaded that any outbreak would spread quickly to the Soviet Union itself, they maintain that "the possibilities of armed intervention by the Soviet bureaucracy (supposing it is still in power) would be measured not so much by the number of tanks and planes in its possession, but by the intensity of class conflict inside the USSR." Most East Europeans are nowhere as certain as this, but they have ceased to consider armed intervention by the Soviet Union inevitable. Future attitudes will depend in part, of course, on what happens in Asia: should the Soviet Union become involved in an armed conflict with China, the chances of its intervening to prevent changes in Eastern Europe would become almost nil in the eyes of the East Europeans.

What then are the alternatives for Eastern Europe? The choice seems wider than in the Soviet Union itself, making predictions even more difficult.

Everything indicates a growing pressure on the Communist parties for greater freedom and more extensive economic and social reforms. Faced with such demands, how will the ruling bureaucracies react? Their likeliest attitude will be to make some concessions but to try to limit them as much as possible, to take two steps forward and one backward, never forgetting that a period of concession and relaxation is usually the most dangerous for a dictatorship: it was during such a period of liberalization that the East German revolt, the Poznan events, and the Hungarian revolution took place.

Yet, the East European Communists may find it more difficult than the Kremlin to keep changes and concessions under strict control. They will be faced with demands which are not, as yet, likely to be put to the Soviet rulers. For example, Djilas's demand for a two-party system is not yet heard in the Soviet Union, but it is openly discussed in Czechoslovakia.

The return to a Stalinist system of coercion cannot be excluded in Eastern Europe any more than in the Soviet Union, although it may seem a remote possibility. Here again, much will depend on developments in Asia. Should the Kremlin be able to reestablish its supremacy there, it may feel able to tell the East European leaders to resist demands for reforms and to suppress opposition by every possible means. On the other hand, however unlikely it may appear today, one cannot exclude the possibility that the Kremlin, preoccupied by the conflict with China, may come to the conclusion that it must have peace and tranquility at its European borders, and that this would be best guaranteed by having autonomous neighbors like Finland instead of discontented satellites.

A few years ago it seemed that Moscow might one day accept the Finnish solution for the East European states because of the danger that the Communist states might fall under the influence of China and become its allies against Russia, just as Albania did. A democratic, neutral, and friendly Finland is certainly preferable to a Communist— but hostile—Albania. But this possibility now seems to have practically vanished; there will hardly be any new Albanias. Still, the Finnish solution may appear to the men in the Kremlin a lesser evil than chaos and violent upheaval, which would become a real threat in the case of Soviet involvement in Asia.

Another possibility is what could be called the Rumanian solution: a regime unwilling to make concessions could try instead to gain popular support by appealing to nationalist and anti-Russian feelings. The result would be a kind of nationalist Balkan dictatorship. It could work for a time. But, as already noted, few Eastern European rulers are likely to follow Rumania's example.

Whether changes in Eastern Europe take place through peaceful evolution or through violent upheaval depends on factors unknown today, such as the future of Sino-Soviet relations, and also on what Mr. Robert Conquest has so aptly called the accidents of history. But there can be little doubt that changes of major significance are bound to come.

Roads to the Future

✳

MERLE FAINSOD

A review of the discussion precipitated by Professor Brzezinski's provocative article reveals two fundamentally different perspectives on the future of the Soviet regime. On
the one hand, there are those who align themselves with
Michel Garder, though not necessarily with his timetable,
in predicting that the regime is doomed to collapse. They
believe that the party leadership finds itself in a prerevolutionary situation where it is faced with insoluble problems
that cannot be resolved within the framework of the existing
political system. They argue that it will inevitably be swept
away by the dynamic social forces with which it has lost
touch. On the other hand, there are those who predict that
the regime will follow a path of evolutionary development,
transforming itself in response to the new challenges which
it faces. They see its problems as serious, but in no sense
posing a fundamental threat to the stability of the regime.
They anticipate that the regime will continue to muddle
along, patching up compromises and adjustments, and re-
sponding sufficiently to the aspirations of its people to avoid
total collapse.

Professor Brzezinski's attitude toward these two contrasting perspectives is somewhat ambiguous. His analysis of the present position implies a crisis of major proportions: an unstable leadership which is "inimical to talent and hostile to political innovation," "a reopening of the gap that existed in prerevolutionary Russia between the political system and the society," an ideology which is increasingly irrelevant to Soviet realities, and the absence of a program to justify party rule. He does not "entirely" exclude "the possibility of revolutionary outbreaks." At the same time he does not affirm the apocalyptic thesis that the regime is destined for catastrophic collapse. He suggests that the ruling Soviet elite can still save itself from the threat of systemic degeneration by co-opting "a broader representation of social talent within the top political leadership," by institutionalizing the selection and tenure of the chief executive, and by giving the institutional and group interests that now exist in Soviet society a more effective representational role. His advice to the party "to adjust gracefully to the desirability, and perhaps even inevitability, of its own gradual withering away" is hardly likely to be warmly embraced by those to whom it is rendered. In any case, Professor Brzezinski avoids identifying himself with the view that such an evolution will or must take place. He does, however, conclude that it represents the only alternative to the degeneration of the Soviet system.

Professor Brzezinski is wise in eschewing prophecy. In the half-century since the establishment of Bolshevik power, there have been innumerable predictions of its imminent collapse, and the discussion inspired by Professor Brzezinski's article indicates that the spate has not abated. Certainly anyone at all sensitive to the role of change in human affairs must recognize that the Soviet regime, like all others, faces the alternatives of adaptation or disintegration and dissolution. While no one can be certain what the future may bring, it is dangerous to assume that the Soviet regime has exhausted the possibilities of adaptation and survival.

However repugnant the Soviet regime may be to Western onlookers, or to disaffected elements in its own population, it is important to recognize the sources of its strength and durability. It has enlisted leading elements of Soviet society in party ranks, even though party functionaries still dominate the leadership. It has consolidated its control over key posts in government, the police, and the armed forces, penetrated important social formations, survived a series of succession crises, and achieved the kind of legitimacy which derives from an impressive record of industrial progress, military victories, territorial gains, and, more recently, an increasing degree of responsiveness to the welfare aspirations of its own people. By abandoning mass terror and placing greater reliance on incentives and amenities, it has sought to narrow the gap between rulers and ruled and to broaden its base of popular support. Faced with rising ferment among intellectuals and students, it has undertaken to quiet restiveness by enlarging the area of permissible criticism while reserving its negative sanctions for the heretics and the heterodox.

As the appeal of its revolutionary ideology has dimmed, it has placed greater reliance on the cementing force of nationalism and anchored its power on the vested interests of the new class bred by industrialization. In contrast with the Communist regimes of Eastern Europe, which bear the stigma of having been established as Soviet client states and which seek their legitimacy in emancipation from Soviet controls, the Soviet regime has been able to draw strong support from identification with a native fund of patriotic sentiment.

In contrast with its Communist Chinese neighbor, which has still to demonstrate its potential for rapid industrialization and which is caught up in the convulsions of frustrated revolutionary expectations and its first succession crisis, the Soviet regime has emerged as a relatively mature industrial power with a broadening social infrastructure involved in its conservation and survival.

Stable as the regime may appear to be, the same cannot be said of the prerogatives of the party functionaries who man the key posts in the party machine and who reserve for themselves the power to define the regime's policy. Limitations on their authority have been imposed by the very revolution over which they have presided. In directing a complex industrial society and in determining its priorities of development, they must increasingly depend on those who possess the professional skills to guide and manage it. In inescapable fashion, the professionalisms of military technology, industrial management, and every branch of science and engineering, impinge on the capacity of the party leadership to coordinate them. Within the ranks of the party there is a continuously troublesome problem of relating the overall authority of full-time party functionaries to the jurisdiction of other party members who exercise professional authority in specialized fields.

As Soviet society has become more professionalized and differentiated, the outlines of an interest-group structure have begun to emerge. The armed forces, the police, the managers of industry and agriculture, the scientific community, and the cultural intelligentsia—all have their specialized interests to defend, and since they cannot be promoted outside the party, the party has itself become an arena in which these competing interests must be adjusted and reconciled. One of the results has been to introduce a strong adaptive ingredient into the party leadership's mobilizing and coordinating role.

There are still other forces at work which contribute to limit, if not to undermine, the authority of the party functionaries and the party which they direct. As the custodians of a doctrine which claims to embody infallible truth, they find their credentials contemptuously rejected by their powerful Chinese neighbor, and they no longer speak for a united Communist world. As spokesmen for the "wave of the future," they see their revolutionary dynamism arrested, and their expansionist ambitions limited by the imperatives of survival in a thermonuclear age. As the putative possessors of an exclusive formula for rapid industrialization, they have watched their growth rate slacken as planning and management problems have become increasingly difficult and complex. Even where they have relaxed restrictions on the cultural intelligentsia and gone part way to satisfy popular expectations of higher living standards, they discover that the appetites which they have whetted demand still more.

What do these developments portend for the future of the Soviet one-party system? There are some who see these pressures as operating to transform what was once a monolithic party into a pluralistic party in which interest groups will be free to maneuver and legalized factions may emerge. There are others who foresee the eventual appearance of a two-party or multi-party system as the leadership finds it impossible to confine the plural energies of Soviet society within the bounds of a single party. There are still others who predict that a weakening of party leadership will set the stage for a military coup d'etat and the emergence of a military dictatorship. There are yet others who visualize the gradual transformation of what was once a militant ideologically-inspired party into a technical and managerial elite, governing in authoritarian fashion, but presiding over an essentially nationalist state.

Without undertaking to predict the shape of things to come, it is, nevertheless, possible to identify certain forces which are likely to influence the development of the Soviet one-party system in the years ahead.

First, it can safely be posited that a party leadership which has built up its power through the suppression of opposition outside the party and of organized factionalism within will not willingly abdicate its supreme role short of a major catastrophe, such as military defeat or an equivalent domestic disaster. Second, it can also be assumed that no party, whatever its pretensions to monolithism, can escape individual and group rivalries, and that these rivalries will inevitably reflect the changing configuration of interests inside the party as they are shaped by the tasks it assumes. Third, in ministering to the needs and directing the destinies of a highly industrialized country, the Soviet leadership must perforce accord greater weight and authority to those in the party who possess the knowledge and technical skills which make an industrial society work. Fourth, as the economy and the society become more complex and differentiated, the influence of professionalism will probably increase, and tendencies toward a dispersal of authority are likely to become more clearly manifest. Fifth, given the commitment of the Soviet regime to technical progress and scientific advance, the need for a social environment conducive to innovation and creativity is likely to intensify and to exert its effect outside scientific walls. Finally, the disillusionment bred by the Sino-Soviet dispute and the spread of polycentric tendencies in the Communist movement, with its self-evident lesson that there are not one, but many Communist truths, should contribute to undermine the dogmatic certainty on which party monolithism rests. If these propositions have any validity, they would point to the emergence over time of a looser, more pragmatic, and pluralistically-based party in which the differentiated interests of an industrial society find freer expression and where the party leadership acts as the manager of their inter-relationships and as the custodian of the national interests of the Soviet state.

There is, of course, no guarantee that future party leaders will respond to the changing social aspirations of an increasingly industrialized and professionalized society or that they will relate themselves creatively to the variety of interests which it has been spawning. They may choose to ignore them. Should they do so, they can only end by sowing the seeds of their own downfall.

The Evolution
of the Soviet System

✳

ARRIGO LEVI

At a September 1966 meeting of Western and East European economists on "Pricing and Planning in Eastern Europe,"[1] the discussions were so open and stimulating, the sense of communication so alive and sweeping, that one of the Western participants was heard to say: "The schism is over. All that remains to be done is to eliminate the consequences."

The impression that the "schism" between East and West is indeed over has gained ground in Europe. This ideological, historical, and political schism has divided parties, peoples, and states. Its resolution would constitute the prelude to a restoration of the geographic and moral unity of Europe, a reunification of the European left, the definitive end of the cold war, and possibly a new era of cooperation between the United States and the Soviet Union. Is it to be wondered, then, that this prospect is seized upon with enthusiasm as much by the intellectual and the politician as by the man on the street?

[1] Meeting of the Center for Economic Studies and Research on Social Problems, held in Florence, Italy, September 1966.

Yet, if the enthusiasm of many is understandable, so surely are the caution and skepticism entertained by others. Is the schism really over? Has the historico-ideological challenge of the Communist world to the non-Communist world actually come to an end? Has the nature of the Communist regimes truly undergone such radical change? Many students and observers of communism incline toward a negative answer, claiming that nothing can change in the Communist world as long as the Communist parties in power remain monolithic and totalitarian. Undoubtedly, the "Leninist" party has changed very little, if at all. Even though the economic reforms have been vast, and obvious shifts in real power have resulted therefrom, political power remains firmly in the hands of the party.

The optimistic belief in the "end of the schism" and the pessimistic view of the "unchangeable nature of party rule" are reflected in the current debate over "evolution or revolution" of the Communist regimes. The optimists are proponents of the evolutionary theory who believe in the capacity of the parties to adapt themselves to new conditions; the pessimists feel that tensions will build up in Communist societies to such a point that the existing political order will explode.

Ten years ago Milovan Djilas raised the vital question of how the totalitarian "new class" society would adapt itself to change. Recently another Yugoslav writer, Mihajlo Markovic, rephrased the question as follows:

An underdeveloped, preeminently rural society . . . cannot avoid that phase of its development in which an elite, in the best of cases a genuinely revolutionary elite, will try to create, through maximum mobilization of the masses and the use of coercion, the conditions necessary [for socialist self-government]—that is to say, an industry, a working class, an intelligentsia, a school system and a mass culture. . . . However, a question arises: when those conditions have been attained, will this elite find the moral strength to decide voluntarily to go on to the essential part of the socialist revolution, namely, the establishment of self-government and, consequently, its own gradual elimination as a power elite? Or will a few decades of intense power concentration have changed its social structure to the point where it will want to be the personification of socialism, to preserve its political and material privileges forever, and to be not only the brain but also the iron fist of the historical process?[2]

This is indeed the paramount question facing the Communist regimes of today. However, Markovic describes here only the most recent phase of the revisionist process, which has barely begun. Before engaging in any attempts to prognosticate the course of this process, we must first have a clearer understanding of the initial revisionist phase which made its appearance immediately upon Stalin's death.

Politics After Stalin

If Stalin's power machine—or political "superstructure," to use a Marxist term—was admirably suited to the conditions of a largely agricultural and only incipiently industrial society, such as Russia was in the 1920s and early 1930s, it had become decidedly anachronistic by the time of its creator's demise, when Russia had already transformed itself into a powerful industrial as well as socially and culturally more sophisticated state. Indeed, March 5, 1953, witnessed not only the passing of an omnipotent dictator, but also the collapse of his political "superstructure." Revisionism thus be-

[2] Mihajlo Markovic, "Socialism and Self-government," in *Critica Marxista*, May-June 1966 (reproduced from *Praxis* of Zagreb).

gan at Stalin's bier. Almost overnight, his successors were faced with the task of maintaining stability, which until then had depended on one man, his instruments of terror, and his myth. Not surprisingly, they decided first to create a meaningful contract between the government and the party and to reassure, not the masses, but the ruling elite (which in a way had suffered more under Stalin's purges) that their "rights" would be respected. This was the fundamental but often disregarded meaning of Khrushchev's secret speech at the 20th Party Congress. The denunciation of Stalin's crimes represented a constitutional charter under which the new leader pledged himself not to use terror. As a guarantee of this pledge, he destroyed the myth of the *Vozhd* (leader). The masses, however, had to wait another five years, until the 22nd Party Congress in 1961, for the myth to be destroyed in public.

Within five or six years after Stalin's death, the new political system managed to achieve substantial stability. The sense of relief that swept over the Soviet Union in the early years of destalinization provided the release of enormous amounts of creative energy, reflected to some degree in Khrushchev's optimistic vitality and zealous patriotism. Despite the occasional signs that destalinization was following a rather "pendular course"—representing a constant struggle between "liberals" and "conservatives"—the Soviet leader's "Bureaucratic Revolution" produced welcome changes in the power system, some of the more significant being:

1. The disappearance of massive and arbitrary terror and the restoration of a certain amount of personal security and respect for law. The laws, to be sure, remained harsh, and were designed to guarantee the authority of the party and to prevent any manifestation of dissent, but at least laws and

regulations took over where unchecked terror and personal vendetta had prevailed before.

2. A change in the ratio of investment for capital goods vs. consumption in favor of consumption, and a consequent improvement in living standards.

3. A rise in agricultural production and a concomitant rise in the living conditions of almost half of the Soviet Union's population—the peasants.

4. A steady improvement in the relations between the political elite and the intellectuals. For the first time in many years, the party found itself faced with the task of having to answer criticism, however cautiously expressed.

5. Freer debate in the highest party echelons, contributing to the development of an oligarchy. (It should be noted, however, that power within the party became concentrated in the Presidium and even more so in the hands of Khrushchev, who exercised absolute control over all information and propaganda, and who more than once appealed to the masses over the heads of the party bureaucrats to maintain his leading position.)

The bureaucratic revolution thus produced a new situation, a kind of managerial state of the "new class" (as Djilas would later describe it) which was certainly preferable to the despotism of "the years of arbitrariness" (*godi proizvolia*)—as Russians referred to the years of Stalin's great purges. To speak of "socialism," or of democracy, during this period would, in this writer's opinion, be manifestly absurd. Yet farfetched though it may sound, there are signs of precisely this phenomenon—a transformation to democratic socialism —manifesting themselves in the second phase of the revisionist process. Fifty years after the October revolution and fourteen years after Stalin's death, one is finally justified in speaking of the halting beginnings of a system which the Revolution was designed to usher in half a century ago.

A Temporary Solution

Khrushchev, to his credit, did manage to assure a peaceful transition between Stalin's despotism and a new balance of power. Under his leadership, the party was able for a time to control the tensions and aspirations toward greater autonomy which appeared in Soviet society after the end of the terror. But just as Stalinism fell victim to its own limitations, so did Khrushchev's bureaucratic solution, with all its appalling shortcomings, generate its own downfall. Khrushchev himself was aware of these shortcomings and limitations—so much so that, in an effort to overcome them, he increasingly accentuated the personal character of his power, as if he alone could grasp, sum up, synthesize, and solve all the problems of Soviet society. "Who will speak out if I don't?" he asked at Minsk in January 1962 in one of his speeches on the state of Soviet agriculture.

The first and principal defect was that on the one hand the new system continually gave rise to aspirations for freedom and well-being on the part of the intellectuals, the technocrats, and ultimately the masses, while on the other it proved incapable of accommodating them in any meaningful, durable fashion. The citadel of power was thus constantly besieged by forces that sought to break in and share power. These forces had to be placated at first, but ultimately repulsed.

Second, the new political solution was extremely shortsighted. For example, the relationship between the party and the *samoupravlenie* (self-government) organs was defined at the time of the 22nd Party Congress as follows:

The building of the Communist society does not occur spontaneously, although it is governed by objective laws. An ever-greater function to that end belongs to the conscious activity of the workers, oriented toward a precise goal and directed by a single will. . . . From it follows the need to broaden even more the task of the Marxist-Leninist party, which is the leading and cognizant force in the construction of communism. It is precisely the party, armed with a scientific theory and attentive to what takes place, which learns . . . more thoroughly and completely the objective tendencies of life so as to direct the creative work of the popular masses. . . . As the state gradually transfers some of its functions to the social organizations, the party increasingly becomes the overall leader of society, and the force that guides the social organizations. Thus, the party also directs the process of the extinction of the state, the activities of the labor unions and other social organizations, whose new tasks it helps to perform on the eve of the advent of communism. . . . The task of the party becomes greater . . . as the party assumes more and more of the functions of organizer and leader of the masses. . . .[3]

In the face of these dicta, the more liberal forces in Soviet society could never make demands based on the principle of *samoupravlenie*. In fact, they opposed it on juridical grounds, holding that it was an instrument of illegality. Rather, they seized on the principle of "socialist legality" in the hope of strengthening the state machinery by making it the natural vehicle for greater freedoms. As B. P. Kravtsov, a liberal Soviet jurist, wrote,

The full development and further improvement of Soviet democracy presupposes the explicit and full proclamation of the people's

[3] *Les principes du Marxisme-Leninisme* (*The Principles of Marxism-Leninism*) Moscow, pp. 691-92.

sovereignty, that is, its primacy and complete dominion. . . . In a state belonging to all the people, it is essential to establish new channels and new forms of participation by the working masses in the performance of state functions: participation in the legislative power, in administration, in enforcing the laws, in supervising their application and exercising control over the activities of the state organs. . . .[4]

However, as long as legality stopped at the doors of the party organization, as long as the party itself remained beyond the rule of law, it was obvious that any meaningful democratization could not take place. The system of power, therefore, was open to easy criticism. The struggle for autonomy on the part of intellectuals, workers, and farmers met with only limited success. Toward the end of the Khrushchev era, in, open criticism of the "alienated Soviet party" began to become commonplace.[5]

Because of this, the enthusiasm that had revived the energy and initiative of Soviet society in the very early years of the post-Stalin era gradually subsided. For example, in the countryside the beneficial effect of the first reforms disappeared after a few years. "Non-collaboration" began anew, and production indices fell. The setback, however, was not so much economic as it was political, in that it showed the limited degree of loyalty that Khrushchev's bureaucratic system was capable of stimulating among the masses, who felt their grievances justified.

Further, there is no doubt that the material sacrifices which the people were called upon to endure were not popular.

[4] Quoted by U. Cerroni in "Constitutional issues in the Soviet Union," *Problems of Socialism*, July-August 1963, p. 872.

[5] See particularly, G. Boffa, *Dopo Krusciov (After Khrushchev)*, Rome, 1965; and V. Strada, *Letteratura Sovietica (Soviet Literature)*, Rome, 1964.

Many thought of them unnecessary, imposed—as they seemed to have been—for ideological reasons. To repress these manifestations of dissent, Khrushchev wasted energy that could have been used elsewhere and lost consensus where he might have found it. All this was, of course, the result of Khrushchev's particular power system and of its internal contradictions.

But it was particularly in the economic field that the bureaucratic system showed its limitations most concretely. The history of Khrushchev's economic reforms is a maze of contradictory measures, of which we need cite only a few.

The seesawing of reform measures, first demanding decentralization and then calling for the consolidation of economic decision-making, was to a great extent more apparent than real. In substance, the determination of economic policy remained the responsibility of the bureaucrats during the entire period. It mattered little if at times control moved from the central ministerial bureaucracy to that of the periphery, or vice versa. The producers, the managers of the *kolkhozes*, and the consumers always remained the objects of manipulation, the executors of the plans, rather than the originators of decisions.

The system, which was nothing more than a continuation of the authoritarian Stalinist type of central planning, became less and less efficient as the Soviet economy grew and as the share of the total production represented by consumers' goods increased. The "purchase plan" for consumers' goods proved to be the most difficult to implement. When the consumers began to show a reluctance to buy, there was no way to force them to do so.

The crisis of the bureaucratic planned economy manifested itself in various ways: in declining growth rates for both industry and agriculture; in the food shortages that resulted from the failure of the agricultural program; in the techno-logical-scientific lag of Soviet industry in many important sectors (electronics, chemistry, etc.), which portended even greater difficulties in the future; and finally in the increasing apathy and cynicism of the population. The Soviet leaders eventually realized that they had to inject greater vitality into the economy than the bureaucratic system had pro-duced. The question was how.

A New Dispensation

The search for an answer to this question began with the proposal to alter the "command economy." It was at this point that the new phase of revisionism took place, for the economic reforms, if fully carried out, promised to impair and curtail radically the economic and political powers of the bureaucracy and the party. From the very beginning, therefore, opponents of the reforms proposed by Liberman, Nemchinov, and others pointed to the danger that the power of the party would seriously diminish once it relinquished any part of its control over the economy.

Hence the caution with which the first experiments in in-dependent management were made, and the fragile compro-mise between the opposing concepts in the solution that was finally adopted. Under the "market apparatus" formula which the Soviets adopted, powers of decision were redis-tributed among producers and consumers, but only in those industrial sectors that produce consumers' goods, with the further essential institutional limitation that the highest or-gans of power would continue to set prices.

This essential point—the continued fixing of prices from above—distinguishes the Soviet economic reforms from those planned in Czechoslovakia, for example, and even more so from the radical liberalization measures adopted in Yugoslavia, which reestablish market mechanisms in the sectors of capital investments and foreign trade. In short, Soviet planning continues to be authoritarian, with little diminution of the economic powers of the state.

The new "socialist market" system "based on the profit of the enterprise" cannot properly be evaluated until its effects have had an opportunity to manifest themselves. Until now, however, the very cautious approach of the Soviet regime in devising compromise formulas makes such an eventuality a rather long-range prospect. In the meantime, however, even a partial market apparatus can set in motion some very strong tensions capable of throwing the entire system out of balance as soon as it discloses the weaknesses that have thus far remained concealed.

Yugoslavia's experience, for example, demonstrates that economic reform can accomplish a great deal, but only at great expense; that it causes and requires radical changes in habits and thinking; and that the profitability of enterprises is not what the masses want unless they have a share in the profits. Weaknesses inherent in the bureaucratic system are bound to reappear. It is true that some of the disadvantages will be offset by a better distribution of decision-making power, greater prosperity, higher wages, and a greater availability of consumer goods on the market. But all this will require a much more open political dialogue between the leaders and the masses, and will eventually impose a different type of political balance.

The Next Step

From forces favorable to development, the conditions of production now become obstacles to these forces.... A period of social
revolution then begins. . . . With the change of the economic
foundation, the entire immense superstructure is more or less
rapidly overthrown.[6]

The classical revolutionary situation thus described by Marx
with reference to the historic surmounting of the "conditions
of production" in proto-capitalism bears a striking resem-
blance to the "conditions of production" in the bureaucratic
society of proto-communism. The intuition underlying the
Marxian theory which attributes autonomy and priority to
economic facts as opposed to political facts seems to find a
whole series of empirical confirmations in the Communist
world of today, where an evolution of the economic system
is taking place independently and cannot be stopped, even
though it is presently curbed by "an immense superstructure" of political roadblocks.

In more general terms, one might say that a modern economic system, because of its internal requirements, tends to
have an organizational and managerial "superstructure" that
is much more complex than is usually permitted under an
authoritarian planning system. A modern economy can function at its best only in a political environment which will
afford the fullest information, the most independent and
unprejudiced research, the most exhaustive and unrestricted
debate. In short, a modern economy can mature only in
some sort of democratic political system.

[6] Karl Marx, *Critique of Political Economy*, London, 1904.

A practical confirmation of these ideas can be found in Eastern Europe. Here the economic reformers are the real revolutionaries. Although they are still searching for a dialogue with the masses and for a suitable base of political independence, they are already clashing with the privileged political circles. The authoritarian and hierarchic structures of the Communist parties and their domineering presence in every aspect of life are hampering the spread of these new autonomies.

This is why it is legitimate to ask whether or not the economic reforms can prevail without a concomitant reform in the party organizations and whether the latter reform does not in turn presuppose some sort of politico-economic crisis.

Even if we agree that the transformation of the economic structures will ultimately "overthrow the political superstructures, gradually or suddenly," we are still far from certain as to how this can actually happen. How far must a political reform be taken for the economic reform to produce the necessary results? How long can the party preserve its antidemocratic and hierarchic structure, or will it be able to renovate this structure with the necessary speed? Up to what point will the autonomous centers of power outside the party be allowed to develop? How will the dialogue between the authorities and the *pays légal* be changed? Lastly, how will the "immense political superstructure" be overthrown, gradually or suddenly?

Good sense tells us that at least at the present stage of our knowledge of social matters, and in the face of the incredible complexity of the power relationships in any society, there are no rational, precise, sure, demonstrable answers to questions of this type. Nevertheless, some salient facts present themselves for consideration.

First, the entire revisionist movement at present revolves around the economic reforms now under way in the Soviet Union and the other countries in Eastern Europe. The most important innovative forces are fighting today for these reforms.

Second, the evolution of the political "superstructure" has not stopped, but is continuing. Although the tempo of the evolution is slow in the Soviet Union, given the prudence and the power of the post-Khrushchev leaders, there is evidence of a gradual power shift from the party to the state organs. (The sphere of state power comprises, let us not forget, the technicians and the business managers.) Therefore, there is a marked "superstructural" difference between Khrushchev's bureaucratic society, hinged as it was to the power of the party bureaucracy, and the bureaucratic society of Brezhnev and Kosygin, in which the party shares power with the technical and state organs. Even some changes in the "philosophy" of the leading group have taken place, particularly with respect to its relationship with the outside world. As to the relationship between the leading group and the country, it continues in large measure to be severely paternalistic, but is nevertheless slowly becoming more and more open and more rational. Prosperity and "rationalization" remain the primary goals of the regime.

Third, if we extend our investigation of revisionism to include the other countries of Eastern Europe, we can clearly see that the innovating process ultimately involves the party, its internal organization, its function in society, and its ideology. The example of Yugloslavia is particularly germane. It seems, in other words, that one can recognize a continuous thread leading from the first manifestations of revisionism (destalinization, the "thaw" in the cold war) to the latest

Yugoslav proposals for radical reforms in the theories of Marx and Lenin, in which ideas of such diverse origins as the social-democratic thought of Kautsky, the communism of Bukharin or Trotsky, and the principles of Western liberal democracy converge.

If we concede that there is a radically new situation in the Soviet Union and Eastern Europe, we must reject as schematic, formal, and overly pessimistic those concepts which maintain that there can be no meaningful change as long as the totalitarian and monolithic nature of the party remains intact. Real power can be subtly redistributed through gradual reforms, while leaving apparently unchanged and unchangeable the absolute power of the bureaucratic hierarchy. This, in effect, has already begun to happen.

Proponents of the theory that the necessary changes in the Soviet Union can come about only through revolution have not paid attention to all the realities of the Communist world, though they do us a service by dramatizing the monolithic nature of the system. It is probably true that the quest for ever greater efficiency, progress, and material comfort (a tendency shared by all contemporary societies in both the East and the West), is related to the growth of democracy and requires the active participation of all business, labor, and professional groups in the making of decisions to a greater extent than is possible under the rigid post-Stalin political system. At the same time, whether we assume that the system will be swept away or that it will accommodate itself to new realities, we must remember that there may be substantial delays along the road—periods of stagnation and lulls during which the innovating fervor may subside or even die out. The fact is that order and security also have their merits for society as a whole. All this works in favor of an evolutionist hypothesis—reinforced, as it is in this author's opinion, by the fact that evolution has been going on in Soviet society for more than a decade.

The evolution of the Soviet power system is continuing. The Communist world is in motion. Old dogmas are being discussed—and frequently discarded—in all the East European countries. The era of myths and ironclad ideologies is coming to an end, and this is the fundamental fact to be noted. How far this process will go is still difficult to say, for we are dealing with not one but several totalitarian societies, each with its own special set of problems, traditions, and goals.

It is encouraging and stimulating to know that the eastern half of Europe is again engaged, however haltingly and in the face of much resistance, in a critical search for new forms of political and economic organization, just as Western Europe is seeking new forms to institutionalize what has been called the "permanent bourgeois revolution." This is what the Western economist meant when he said, "The schism is over." Looking East, we no longer see a blank wall, but new political horizons. This is certainly much more than we might have hoped for just over ten years ago, when Soviet troops crushed the Hungarian rebellion.

Concluding Reflections

ZBIGNIEW BRZEZINSKI

To any student of Soviet affairs, myself included, the critical reactions to the discussion initiated by Mr. Tatu's and my essays provide an extraordinary wealth of stimulating insights, alternative ways of looking at the problem, and different assessments of existing trends. Accordingly, it would be taking unfair advantage to use this last word just to defend my viewpoint. Rather, it might be more appropriate to use these remarks to indicate very briefly and selectively in what way I now feel I should reevaluate my original position as well as to develop some of my views in the light of the comments made in the symposium. Perhaps a helpful way to begin would be to remind the reader what my initial thesis was, at least as I understand it.

Decay and Reform

In my estimate, the Soviet Communist party, having been for some years the source of social innovation, has now become a brake on social progress within the Soviet Union. The Soviet society has acquired the wherewithal for further growth, and the bureaucratic and dogmatic restraints imposed on it by the ruling party have become dysfunctional to that growth. Thus a gap is opening between the society and the Soviet political system, in some ways reminiscent of the late Tsarist period. This condition is aggravated by a decline in the quality of the Soviet political elite, and by the growing assertiveness of various other key groups. These groups can reason quite legitimately that ideological, party, and police controls make much less sense today than they did when Soviet society was still in the process of being deliberately shaped by the political system. The political elite, increasingly bureaucratized, self-centered, and aging,[1] is unable to respond effectively either through terror or reform. The result is stagnation—which, unless corrected by major institutional reforms, will lead to degeneration.

In his very thoughtful essay, Professor Barghoorn took me to task both for being somewhat vague in defining decay and for propounding reforms for the Soviet political system clearly beyond the reach and the will of the present Soviet elite. With respect to the first, decay is necessarily a rather ambiguous term. In general, what I meant by it is the system's growing incapacity to confront major domestic issues resiliently and its inability to attract into the ranks of the political elite the ablest, most energetic, and innovative elements of society (a point well made in Mr. Galli's contribution). Perhaps the best formulation for this development is Mr. Conquest's succinct statement: "The political system is radically and dangerously inappropriate to its social and economic dynamics."

---

[1] The average age of Central Committee members is close to 60—which makes the top Soviet elite about the oldest in any major modern state.

As for the second point, Professor Barghoorn—and also Professor Fainsod—are quite justified in their skepticism concerning the willingness of the regime to undertake the far-reaching reforms that I said were needed. What in fact I intended to convey was that precisely because the necessary reforms are so major in scope, it is unlikely that they will be implemented, at least in the foreseeable future.

The Soviet party bureaucracy, like any groups of men in authority, finds it easy to justify its monopoly of power, while its ideology further reassures it that no basic change in the political set-up is in the collective interest of Soviet society. Thus the ruling bureaucracy, I fear, will oppose any efforts to loosen the grip of the party on Soviet society and to increase the range of social autonomy. It is always easier to rationalize the proposition that you need to hang on to the maximum of political power than to accept the notion that in fact you ought to devolve power unto others. History is full of precedents of a political elite being blind to its country's real needs and real interests. It is for these very reasons that I lean toward the stagnation-degeneration pattern.

Reactionary Palace Coup

Where I would differ more strongly with Professor Barghoorn is with respect to his view that "if the present Soviet political system disintegrates within the next few years, it will probably be replaced, at least for some time, by a nationalistic oligarchy, representing a coalition of forces, dominated by moderate, production-oriented party leaders, scientists, industrialists, and military figures."

My own feeling is that if continuing stagnation leads to this disintegration, the response will be not a veering toward a "moderate" coalition, but rather a more assertive ideological-nationalist reaction, resting on a coalition of secret police, the military, and the heavy industrial-ideological complex—for example, Shelepin, supported by the "Young Turks."

Thus, in considering the direction of a sudden turn from a broad developmental pattern, even though the probabilities of such a turn cannot be defined precisely, I now find myself closer to the arguments of Mr. Levine and particularly to the conclusion of Mr. Conquest's very perceptive essay. Accordingly, I judge Mr. Lyons's prediction of a revolution less persuasive than the notion of a coup. This is not to gainsay the existence of popular discontent, which in some quarters—particularly among intellectuals—has developed into open political ferment. The fact that profound political issues are being aired in public by dissenting groups is of crucial importance. And in all probability there is more political ferment in the Soviet Union than we are aware of, since we see only the top of the iceberg. Yet, while such destabilizing tendencies are gaining in force and are bound to affect the internal debates within the political leadership, they can hardly be viewed as the prelude to revolution. A revolution in a relatively developed society nowadays requires both the complete paralysis of the government and some definition of an oppositional program, effectively disseminated among the potentially revolutionary masses. Alternatively, it needs a conspiratorial group, capable of inducing social chaos. Thus, a revolution requires many more preconditions than an internal palace coup, brought about by a reaction of some of the ruling elite to growing evidence of political stagnation.

It is true, however, that the emergence, through a palace coup, of a reactionary dictatorship would aggravate Soviet domestic tensions, and would probably strain world peace as well. It would be good neither for the Soviet Union nor for us.

Political Evolution

The preceding considerations make me also somewhat skeptical of Mr. Leonhard's "evolutionary transformation,"[2] Professor Schlesinger's "muddling evolution," Mr. Levi's "rationalist evolution," and finally Dr. Bandyopadhyaya's dialectical "regeneration" through aggravated domestic contradictions. In each case the unanswered question is transformation, or evolution, or regeneration, into what and by whom? I do think that Professor Schlesinger and Dr. Bandyopadhyaya are right in stressing a point I neglected in my original analysis: the impact of international relations on internal Soviet politics. Their feeling is that international stability will speed the evolution. Granting this, one must ask whether it is in fact likely that there will be such stability. My own somewhat pessimistic view is that we will not have much international stability in the 1970s. And if this turns out to be the case, how will the Soviet Union, increasingly capable of playing a major role on the world scene, react to new international conflicts and "Third World" chaos? International trends could have the effect of encouraging a more assertive, ideological-nationalist posture, as mentioned above, in addition to maximizing domestic Soviet difficulties. Having said this, I would still persist in arguing that it is incumbent on the West not to adopt such a negative posture toward the Soviet Union as to make the pessimistic projection a self-fulfilling prophecy.

[2] See Wolfgang Leonhard's "Notes on an Agonizing Diagnosis," *Problems of Communism*, July-August 1966, commenting on Garder's book.

Table

Perhaps a more basic problem in working with the notion of "evolution" is that, unless this "evolution" is specifically defined, it can mean all sorts of things, ranging from stagnation to democratic reformism. A more precise definition of the possible character of the Soviet evolutionary process is to be found in Professor Meissner's and Professor Fainsod's searching essays. Both feel, and I agree, that the party is making adjustments in its system of rule, designed to increase economic efficiency without compromising political power. In the process, the more stringent Stalinist totalitarian qualities of the system are giving way to a somewhat more traditional authoritarian pattern.

Readers may be interested to see charted on a spectrum the views of participants in this symposium, including those who did not comment on my introductory essay and who therefore are not included in this volume. The chart—prepared by Mr. Edward McGowan, a Ph.D. candidate in government at Columbia University, New York—is patterned after my graphic interpretation of the policy positions of Soviet leaders, published with my opening contribution to the symposium. The numbered lines below refer to contributors in order of their appearance in *Problems of Communism*. The positions of the numbers indicate each author's major conclusions regarding the probable direction of change in the Soviet Union's political development. The lines show the range of other predictive alternatives envisaged by the authors.—ZB.

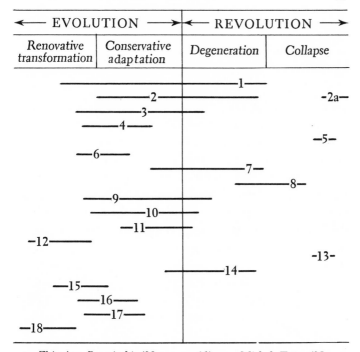

1—Zbigniew Brzezinski (No. 1, 1966). 2—Michel Tatu (No. 2, 1966). 2a—Michel Garder (whose position is discussed by Mr. Tatu, *idem.*). 3—Frederick C. Barghoorn (No. 3, 1966). 4—Wolfgang Leonhard (No. 4, 1966). 5—Eugene Lyons (No. 4, 1966). 6—Arthur Schlesinger, Jr. (No. 4, 1966). 7—Giorgio Galli (No. 5, 1966). 8—Robert Conquest (No. 5, 1966). 9—Hans J. Morgenthau (No. 5, 1966). 10—Boris Meissner (No. 6, 1966). 11—Robert Strausz-Hupé (No. 6, 1966). 12—Jayantanuja Bandyopadhyaya (No. 1, 1967). 13—Isaac Don Levine (No. 1, 1967). 14—Ernst Halperin (No. 1, 1967). 15—Joseph Clark (No. 1, 1967). 16—Sidney Hook (No. 2, 1967). 17—Merle Fainsod (No. 4, 1967). 18—Arrigo Levi (No. 4, 1967).
N.B.: Two contributors to the symposium, Boris Souvarine (No. 2, 1967) and Alexander Bregman (No. 3, 1967), are omitted from the chart since their discussions did not include clear-cut projections for the future.

Economics and Politics

However, the foregoing discussion begs the question: Are these adjustments rapid and extensive enough? My argument would be that the gap between Soviet society and its political system has widened because society has matured and developed more rapidly than the political system. In other words, I would not claim that the political elite or its system is unchanging; I would argue that the changes in Soviet society have been more extensive and more significant than the comparable changes in the character of the Soviet elite. That elite today is certainly more technologically educated than its predecessors were two or three decades ago. Nonetheless, it is still essentially a bureaucratic elite, even though some of its members have more technical skills. Moreover, intellectually it is probably of a lower order than was the case, let us say, thirty years ago. Stalin decimated the elite of that day and installed in power a new generation, recruited essentially from peasants and lower proletarians to whom political power meant also social advancement. It is this generation that today dominates the Soviet Union. I doubt that it is capable of making the kind of creative adjustments that are called for, and which, for example, the Yugoslav political elite seems to be at least considering.

I would also argue that economic reforms, while perhaps creating more favorable conditions for the eventual development of democracy, still require an act of will on the part of the political elite to move in the direction of democratic reformism. By way of example, even in the heyday of Nazi totalitarianism, the economic system was in fact more decentralized than it is today in either the Soviet Union or perhaps Yugoslavia. There is thus no automatic connection between the degree of concentration of the economy and the character of the political system. To be sure, if there is decentralization of the economic system, it is easier, if the political elite so desires, to move on to the next stage of political decentralization. My argument, to make it clear even at the risk of repetition, is that there is nothing automatic about this process. At some point, the Soviet political elite, or more specifically some Soviet leader, will have to decide deliberately that this is the direction in which to head. It is because Tito was able to make this decision, and had sufficient power to override the opposition of his own conservatives, that Yugoslavia has made such impressive progress.

This leads us to a paradox. Precisely because there is today no one in effective power in the Soviet Union, it is even more difficult to make the kind of decisions which a political system occasionally needs to make. The various power groups are today more assertive, the struggles for power are less convulsive, the collective leadership is more collective, and the effect is a kind of partial policy paralysis.

The question for the future is whether this kind of passive consensus can endure. It results in a progressive lowering in the level of effective political control over society, a lowering which has to be matched (if stability is to be maintained) by a corresponding decline in politically-initiated innovation. The alternatives are to permit social groups to initiate innovation —that is, the democratic pattern; to move toward coercive innovation; or to muddle through in-between, at the cost of both innovation and control.[3]

The Nationality Problem

Let me now turn to one issue which I was struck to see neglected by almost all contributors, save the late Mr. Bregman. It involves the question of the non-Russian nationalities. This omission, it seems to me, is indicative of the inclination of many Western scholars of Soviet affairs to minimize what I fear may be potentially a very explosive issue in the Soviet policy. (The "analytical" gap has, felicitously, been narrowed somewhat by the Sept.-Oct. 1967 issue of *Problems of Communism,* devoted entirely to the topic.)

We still live in the age of nationalism, and my own highly generalized feeling is that it is going to be exceedingly difficult for the Soviet Union to avoid having some of its many nationalities go through a phase of assertive nationalism. The non-Russian nationalities are today led by Soviet elites, and precisely because of this they are more effective in pursuing their own national objectives within the framework of the Soviet political system. They can claim such things as politi-

[3] The chart below may be a useful way for synthesizing the relationship between political control and innovation in Soviet experience:

		Political control over society	
		LOW	HIGH
Impact on society of political innovation	LOW	Brezhnev	Lenin
	HIGH	Khrushchev	Stalin

cal autonomy, constitutional reform, a greater share of the national economic pie, more investment, without it appearing that they wish to secede from the Soviet Union. History teaches us, be it in Algeria or in Indonesia or in Africa, that these demands will grow rather than decline. If they are not met or are suppressed, it is likely that the demands will become sharper and more self-assertive. If they are satisfied, they will grow with the eating.

I frankly do not see how the central authorities in the Soviet Union will be able to avoid having a prolonged period of fairly difficult relations with the non-Russian nationalities. I also see no reason why the Ukrainians, or the Uzbeks, or the Georgians, or others may not feel that they ought to have a greater sense of national autonomy to enjoy. If Canada or Belgium cannot escape the central phenomenon of our times, I am unconvinced that the Soviet Union can, and the burden of proof ought to be on those who say that it can. If the problem does continue to develop, the effect could be to produce in the Soviet Union a political issue of even greater proportions than that posed by the current racial crisis in the United States.

Soviet Staying Power

Finally, to end on a highly speculative note: what about the capacity of the Soviet Union to sustain an effective historical challenge to the West, particularly to the United States? It seems that while everything points to a continuing growth in Soviet military power, there is at least a possibility that the Soviet political system, as well as the Soviet economy, may not be able to withstand a protracted rivalry with the United States. The political reasons for this hypothesis have already been indicated, but much will also depend on the rate of Soviet economic growth.

It has been estimated that if the American economy grows by only 3 per cent, by 1985 the U.S. GNP will be somewhere around 1.4 trillion dollars; if it grows by 4.5 per cent, it will be somewhere around 1.7 trillion. On the other hand, if the Soviet GNP grows even at the rate of 5 per cent, by 1985 it will be still under 800 billion dollars. In other words, the gap between the United States and the Soviet Union will almost double. If the Soviet rate of growth should decline to 2 per cent, the Soviet GNP by 1985 will be less than 450 billion, or only one-third that of the United States, and only about as much as that of Japan, assuming that Japan maintains its present impressive rate of growth.

It may be rash for a student of politics to speculate about economics, but this writer cannot suppress the feeling that the Soviet Union will require major internal transformations in its social, economic, and political order if it wishes to maintain rapid technological and economic development. (The more advanced Czechs have just come to this conclusion about their own country.) Our discussion raises at least the possibility that the political system will not be willing to make the necessary adjustments. If the result is both political and economic inefficiency, the Soviet Union would suffer as a world power. On the other hand, if the adjustments are made, the Soviet political system will have to pay the price.

These factors cumulatively give rise to the question: is Russia at the end of the highly motivated energetic period in its history and at the beginning of the sterile bureaucratic phase? Such energetic and then bureaucratic cycles have been typical of Russian history: a major challenge gives rise to a major national response, coercively and collectively organized;

the organized response then in turn becomes fossilized and bureaucratically stagnant, leading to a period of decay.

Yet it would be wrong to take comfort in this possibility. The modern world is today on the eve of a fantastic transformation, with its most advanced societies beginning to leave the industrial era and entering what I have called elsewhere the new technetronic age. It is in the interest of all of mankind that the second major nuclear power does not remain an increasingly antiquated despotism, a vestigial remnant of nineteenth-century ideology and of early industrial bureaucratism, committed to domestic and international goals of fading relevance to the new realities. That is why so much depends on the ability of Soviet society, and particularly of the younger Soviet generation, to overcome the entrenched resistance of a political system that today is uneasy with its past and uncertain of its future.

Bibliographical Note

The articles included in this symposium were taken from the
following issues of *Problems of Communism*:

Brzezinski	January—February 1966
Barghoorn	May—June 1966
Schlesinger	July—August 1966
Lyons	July—August 1966
Galli	September—October 1966
Conquest	September—October 1966
Meissner	November—December 1966
Bandyopadhyaya	January—February 1967
Levine	January—February 1967
Halperin	January—February 1967
Clark	January—February 1967
Bregman	May—June 1967
Fainsod	July—August 1967
Levi	July—August 1967
Brzezinski	May—June 1968

Books Published by the
Research Institute on Communist Affairs

Diversity in International Communism, Alexander Dallin, ed., in collaboration with the Russian Institute, Columbia University Press, 1963.

Political Succession in the USSR, Myron Rush, published jointly with the RAND Corporation, Columbia University Press, 1965.

Marxism in Modern France, George Lichtheim, Columbia University Press, 1966.

Power in the Kremlin from Khrushchev to Kosygin, Michel Tatu, published in French by Grasset, 1966 and in English by Viking Press, 1969.

Vietnam Triangle, Donald Zagoria, Pegasus Press, 1968.

The Soviet Bloc: Unity and Conflict, Zbigniew Brzezinski, revised and enlarged edition, Harvard University Press, 1967.

Communism in Malaysia and Singapore: Its History, Program and Tactics, Justus Van Der Kroef, Nijhoff Publishers, The Hague, 1968.

Radicalismo Cattolico Brasiliano, Ulisse Alessio Floridi, (in Italian) Instituto Editorial Del Mediterraneo, 1968.

Marxism and Ethics, Eugene Kamenka, Macmillan, London, 1969.

Stalin and His Generals, Seweryn Bialer, ed. Pegasus Press, 1969.

Communists and Their Law, John N. Hazard, University of Chicago Press, 1969.

Asian Triangle, Bhabani Sen Gupta, published jointly with the East Asian Institute, Pegasus Press, 1969.

Case Studies in Soviet Foreign Policy: Arming the "Third World", Uri Ra'anan, MIT Press, 1969.